DISCO

TOP 10

SHANGHAI

2024

Colorful Travel Guide

Gerald E. Priddy

Copyright © Gerald E. Priddy, 2024.
All rights reserved. No part of this publication may be reproduced, distributed, or transmitted in any form or by any means, including photocopying, recording, or other electronic or mechanical methods, without the prior written permission of the publisher, except in the case of brief quotations embodied in critical reviews and certain other noncommercial uses permitted by copyright law.

Table of Contents

Why Visit Shanghai   8
Visa Requirements   9

SKYSCRAPERS AND MODERN MARVELS

The Bund   11
Pudong Skyline   12
Shanghai Tower   12
Jin Mao Tower   13
Oriental Pearl Tower   14

CULTURAL ENCLAVES AND HISTORIC SITES

Yuyuan Garden   15
Jade Buddha Temple   16
Shanghai Old Town   16
The Former French Concession   17

ART AND ENTERTAINMENT SCENE

M50 Art District   18
Shanghai Museum   18
Acrobatic Shows and Theaters   19
Shanghai Disney Resort   20

WATERFRONT RETREATS AND PARKS

People's Square   22
Zhongshan Park   22
Century Park   22

CULINARY ADVENTURES

Nanxiang Steamed Bun Restaurant 23
Must Try Street Food in Chenghuangmiao 24
Michelin-starred Restaurants 25
Night Food Markets 27

CLASSIC SHANGHAI IN 3 DAYS

Day 1: The Bund and Pudong 28
Day 2: Yuyuan Garden and Old Town 28
Day 3: French Concession and Art Districts 28

FAMILY-FRIENDLY EXPLORATION

Day 1: Shanghai Disney Resort 30
Day 2: Science and Technology Museums 30
Day 3: Family Parks and Entertainment 30

ARTS AND CULTURE ITINERARY

Day 1: M50 Art District 32
Day 2: Shanghai Museum and Theaters 32
Day 3: Literary Cafes and Bookstores 32

NATURE AND RELAXATION ESCAPE

Day 1: Zhongshan Park 34
Day 2: Suzhou Creek and Waterfront 34
Day 3: Street Food Safari 34

HIDDEN GEMS AND LOCAL FAVORITES

Secret Cafes and Hangouts	37
Offbeat Art Galleries	38
Authentic Local Eateries	39
Non-touristy Souvenir Shops	40

NIGHTLIFE AND ENTERTAINMENT

Rooftop Bars with a View	41
Trendy Nightclubs	42
Traditional Teahouses	43
Night Markets and Events	44

SHOPPING IN SHANGHAI

Luxury Shopping Districts	46
Antique and Vintage Finds	47
Local Designers and Boutiques	48
Bargain Markets	49

ACCOMMODATION RECOMMENDATION

Luxury Hotels with a View	50
Boutique Stays in French Concession	52
Budget-Friendly Hostels	54

WHEN TO VISIT AND WEATHER

Shanghai's Climate	55
Festival Calendar	56
Weather Tips for Different Times	57

GETTING AROUND SHANGHAI

Transportation Options	57
Renting Bicycles and Electric Scooters	59
Essential Phrases for Communication	60

BEATING THE CROWDS

Best Times to Visit Popular Sites	62
Insider Tips for Timing	63
Reservation Strategies	64

CULTURAL INSIGHTS AND ETIQUETTE

Understanding Local Customs	66
Dress Code and Behavior	67
Interacting with Locals	68

SHANGHAI'S HISTORICAL BACKGROUND

Early Settlements and Trade	69
Modern Economic Development	72

ARCHITECTURAL DIVERSITY

Colonial-Era Buildings	76
Art Deco and Modern Structures	77
Arts and Culture Scene	78

RELIGIOUS AND SPIRITUAL HERITAGE

Temples and Shrines	80
Longhua Temple:	81

WHY VISIT SHANGHAI

Shanghai's iconic skyline is a captivating draw. Pudong, the futuristic financial district, showcases a breathtaking array of architectural marvels, including the Oriental Pearl Tower and the Shanghai Tower. As day turns into night, the cityscape transforms into a dazzling sea of lights, casting a spellbinding glow upon the Huangpu River.

Shanghai's rich history is palpable in the Old Town, where ancient temples, narrow alleyways, and the classical Yuyuan Garden transport visitors to a bygone era. The juxtaposition of these historic sites against the backdrop of the city's modern skyline provides a unique glimpse into the cultural evolution of Shanghai.

Culinary enthusiasts find a haven in Shanghai, where a diverse array of street food stalls, traditional teahouses, and fine dining establishments cater to every palate. From the renowned xiaolongbao, a type of soup dumpling, to savory street snacks like scallion pancakes and stinky tofu, the city's gastronomic offerings are a feast for the senses.

Beyond the gastronomic delights, Shanghai is a shopper's paradise. Nanjing Road, one of the world's busiest shopping streets, is lined with luxury boutiques, department stores, and local markets. The city's vibrant markets, such as the trendy Tianzifang, offer a delightful blend of traditional crafts and modern trinkets.

Shanghai's efficient and expansive public transportation system makes exploring the city a breeze. Whether cruising along the Huangpu River, riding the high-speed Maglev train, or navigating the metro system, getting around is convenient and adds to the overall experience.

VISA REQUIREMENTS

Visa requirements and processing for a visit to Shanghai, China, are subject to change, and it's crucial to verify the latest information from official sources. Generally, foreign visitors to China, including Shanghai, are required to obtain a visa before arrival. Here's a brief overview of the typical visa requirements and processing steps:

Determine the Type of Visa:

Tourist Visa (L Visa): For tourism purposes, such as sightseeing, visiting friends or relatives.
Business Visa (M Visa): For business-related activities, including conferences, meetings, or market research.

Application Process:

Contact the Chinese embassy or consulate in your home country to obtain the most up-to-date information and the correct application form.
Fill out the visa application form accurately, providing all required documentation.

Required Documents:

Valid passport with at least six months' validity beyond the intended stay.
Completed visa application form.
Passport-sized photos meeting specific requirements.
Flight itinerary and hotel reservation details.
Proof of financial ability to cover the expenses during the visit.
For business visas, an invitation letter from a Chinese business entity may be required.

Visa Processing Time:

Visa processing times can vary depending on the type of visa and the embassy or consulate. It's advisable to apply well in advance of your planned travel dates.

Submission and Payment:

Submit the completed application form and required documents to the Chinese embassy or consulate.
Pay the visa application fee. Fees can vary based on nationality and type of visa.

Visa Interview:
Some applicants may be required to attend an interview at the embassy or consulate.

Collecting the Visa:
Once the visa is processed, collect it from the embassy or consulate in person or through a designated representative.

Visa Extension:
If you plan to stay in Shanghai for an extended period, you may need to apply for a visa extension within China.

SKYSCRAPERS AND MODERN MARVELS

THE BUND

The Bund, located along the western bank of the Huangpu River, is a historical waterfront area that dates back to the 19th century. It originally served as the financial center of colonial Shanghai and boasts a stunning collection of architectural styles, ranging from Gothic and Baroque to Romanesque. These buildings reflect the city's multicultural past and international influences.

Tourist Engagement:
Tourist Engagement:
Take a leisurely stroll along the promenade to appreciate the architectural marvels, such as the Peace Hotel and the Customs House. Consider a river cruise for a different perspective, especially during the evening when the skyline is illuminated. Numerous cafes and restaurants line the Bund, offering a perfect spot to relax and soak in the atmosphere.
While the Bund is captivating at any time of day, the evening is truly magical as the skyscrapers across the river light up, creating a dazzling display. Sunset provides a beautiful transition from day to night. Keep in mind that weekends can be crowded, so weekdays may offer a more relaxed experience.

Website:
htttps://www.bund18.com/
Phone Number:
+86 21 53083388

PUDONG SKYLINE

Pudong, on the eastern bank of the Huangpu River, was predominantly farmland until the late 20th century when it underwent rapid development. The area is now a symbol of Shanghai's modernity, featuring iconic skyscrapers such as the Shanghai Tower, Jin Mao Tower, and the Oriental Pearl Tower.

Tourist Engagement:

Head to the observation decks of the Shanghai Tower or the Oriental Pearl Tower for breathtaking views of the city. Consider taking a Huangpu River cruise for a panoramic view of the skyline. The Lujiazui area, where many of these skyscrapers are located, also offers high-end shopping and dining experiences.
Visit Pudong in the evening to witness the city lights and the spectacular light show on the facades of the buildings. Early mornings can offer a serene view before the hustle and bustle begins.

Phone Numbers:
+86 21 20656666
Oriental Pearl Tower: +86 21 58791888

Opening Hours:
open around 8:30 AM and close in the evening,

SHANGHAI TOWER

Shanghai Tower, standing proudly in the heart of the Lujiazui financial district, is a marvel of modern architecture and engineering. Completed in 2015, it is the tallest skyscraper in China and the second-tallest in the world. The tower's design incorporates sustainable features, and its spiraling form represents traditional Chinese architecture with a modern twist.

Tourist Engagement:
Embark on a thrilling journey to the top by taking one of the world's fastest elevators, reaching speeds of 18 meters per second.

Once at the observation decks, enjoy breathtaking, unobstructed views of the entire city, the Huangpu River, and the surrounding skyscrapers. Interactive exhibits and multimedia displays provide insights into the tower's construction and Shanghai's dynamic development.

For an extraordinary experience, plan your visit during the late afternoon to witness the city bathed in the warm glow of the setting sun, transitioning into the dazzling lights of the evening skyline. Weekdays typically see fewer visitors, providing a more intimate atmosphere.

Phone Number:
+86 21 2065 666
Opening Hours:
Generally open at 8:30 AM and close in the evening.

JIN MAO TOWER

Nestled in the iconic Lujiazui skyline, the Jin Mao Tower is a testament to Shanghai's architectural prowess. Completed in 1998, it held the title of the tallest building in China until the completion of the Shanghai World Financial Center in 2007. The tower's design combines traditional Chinese architectural elements with a modern aesthetic, symbolizing harmony between the old and the new.

Tourist Engagement:

Take an exhilarating elevator ride to the observation deck on the 88th floor, which offers breathtaking panoramic views of Shanghai. The Skywalk, a glass-floored platform, provides a thrilling perspective of the city below. Explore the Grand Hyatt Shanghai hotel, which occupies the tower's upper floors, and marvel at the intricate details of the tower's interior design.

To capture the cityscape in its full glory, visit Jin Mao Tower in the late afternoon. As the sun sets, witness the transition from daylight to the sparkling lights of Shanghai's skyline. If you enjoy a quieter experience, consider visiting on weekdays to avoid the weekend crowds.

ORIENTAL PEARL TOWER

Rising gracefully along the banks of the Huangpu River, the Oriental Pearl Tower is an iconic symbol of Shanghai's modernity. Completed in 1994, its distinctive design, featuring spheres linked by futuristic columns, has made it a landmark in the city skyline. The tower serves both practical and symbolic purposes, housing observation decks, a hotel, and a revolving restaurant.

Tourist Engagement:

Take a high-speed elevator to the observation decks, located at various heights, for panoramic views of Shanghai. The glass-floored Sky Walk provides an exhilarating experience, allowing you to look down directly at the city below. The tower also features the Shanghai Municipal History Museum, offering insights into the city's transformation over the years.

To witness the mesmerizing city lights, plan your visit to the Oriental Pearl Tower in the evening. The sunset provides a beautiful backdrop, and as darkness falls, the lights of Shanghai create a captivating spectacle. Consider weekdays for a more relaxed experience, as weekends can be busier with tourists.

Phone Number:
+86 21 5879 1888

CULTURAL ENCLAVES AND HISTORIC SITES

YUYUAN GARDEN

Step into the tranquility of ancient China by visiting Yuyuan Garden, a masterpiece of classical Chinese landscaping located in the heart of Shanghai. Built during the Ming Dynasty in the 16th century, this historic garden reflects traditional Suzhou-style landscaping. Explore its intricate pavilions, winding paths, koi-filled ponds, and beautifully curated flora, all surrounded by traditional architecture.

Tourist Engagement:
Wander through the various sections of Yuyuan Garden, each with its own unique charm. Admire the ornate details of the Huxinting Tea House, which sits atop a zigzag bridge over a picturesque pond. Explore the Inner Garden, known for its rockeries and beautifully crafted structures. Don't miss the Yule Pavilion, a central point offering a panoramic view of the entire garden.

Visit Yuyuan Garden in the early morning or late afternoon to avoid the crowds and enjoy a more peaceful atmosphere. Spring, with blooming flowers, or autumn, when the weather is mild, is an ideal time to experience the garden's beauty. Weekdays are generally less crowded compared to weekends.

Website:
https://www.yugarden.com/
Phone Number:
+86 21 6326 0830

JADE BUDDHA TEMPLE

Immerse yourself in the spiritual ambiance of Shanghai by visiting the Jade Buddha Temple, a sacred Buddhist site with a rich history. Built in 1882 during the Qing Dynasty, the temple is renowned for its two exquisite jade Buddha statues imported from Myanmar. The temple complex also includes various halls, pavilions, and beautifully landscaped gardens.

Tourist Engagement:

Marvel at the intricate architecture and serene atmosphere as you explore the different halls within the temple. The highlight is undoubtedly the Jade Buddha Chamber, where the two jade statues, one sitting and one reclining, are enshrined. Witness the devoted worshippers engaging in prayer and rituals, adding to the authentic spiritual experience.

Early morning is the best time to experience the Jade Buddha Temple in a tranquil setting, allowing you to absorb the spiritual energy without the bustling crowds. If you are interested in witnessing Buddhist ceremonies, check the temple's schedule for specific events and festivals.

Phone Number:
+86 21 6266 3668

SHANGHAI OLD TOWN

Step into the charming heart of historic Shanghai by exploring Nanshi, the Old Town. Dating back to the Ming and Qing dynasties, this area preserves the city's traditional architecture and layout. Wander through narrow alleyways, discover ancient temples, and experience the unique blend of Chinese and Western influences that define this historic neighborhood.

Tourist Engagement:
Immerse yourself in the vibrant atmosphere as you stroll through bustling markets and historic streets. Visit the iconic City God Temple, a spiritual center with a history dating back to the 15th century. Explore Yuyuan Garden and the adjacent Yuyuan Bazaar, where you can shop for traditional Chinese crafts and sample local delicacies. Engage with the locals, enjoy street performances, and capture the essence of Old Shanghai.

Late afternoon is an ideal time to experience the Old Town. As the day transitions into evening, the traditional architecture is beautifully illuminated, creating a magical atmosphere. Weekdays are generally less crowded, allowing for a more leisurely exploration.

Phone Number:
+86 21 2311 9911

THE FORMER FRENCH CONCESSION

Step into a harmonious blend of history and modernity as you explore the Former French Concession (FFC) in Shanghai. Established in the mid-19th century, this area served as the French settlement in the city. Today, it stands as a testament to Shanghai's cosmopolitan past, with tree-lined streets, historic villas, and an eclectic mix of boutiques, cafes, and galleries.

Tourist Engagement:
Embark on a leisurely walk or rent a bicycle to explore the tree-shaded avenues and charming alleyways of the FFC. Admire the well-preserved Shikumen architecture, characterized by stone archways and traditional courtyard houses. Engage with the vibrant cultural scene by visiting art galleries, boutiques, and coffee shops. Take a moment to relax in one of the many parks or gardens scattered throughout the area.

The Former French Concession is enchanting throughout the day, but late afternoon and early evening offer a special charm. As the sun sets, the tree-lined streets are bathed in warm hues, and the eclectic mix of shops and cafes comes to life. Weekdays are generally more relaxed, allowing for a quieter exploration.

ART AND ENTERTAINMENT SCENE

M50 ART DISTRICT

Dive into the vibrant contemporary art scene of Shanghai by exploring the M50 Art District. Formerly a textile mill, this area has been transformed into a dynamic hub for local and international artists. The name "M50" comes from the building's address on Moganshan Road and has become synonymous with creativity, innovation, and artistic expression

Tourist Engagement:
Immerse yourself in a plethora of galleries, studios, and exhibition spaces that showcase a diverse range of artworks, from paintings and sculptures to multimedia installations.

with artists at work, attend gallery openings, and gain insights into the ever-evolving Chinese contemporary art scene. The district exudes a bohemian atmosphere, and you'll find a mix of established artists and emerging talents.

Visit M50 Art District during the late morning or early afternoon to enjoy a more relaxed atmosphere. Weekdays are generally quieter, providing ample opportunities to interact with artists and gallery owners. Consider checking the district's event calendar for special exhibitions or events, and plan your visit accordingly.

Website:
http://www.m50.com.cn/
Phone Number:
+86 21 6350 0921
Opening Hours:
10:00 AM to 6:00 PM.

SHANGHAI MUSEUM

Embark on a journey through China's rich cultural heritage by visiting the Shanghai Museum, a treasure trove of ancient artifacts and art spanning thousands of years. Established in 1952, the museum moved to its current location in People's Square in 1996. The building's design, resembling an ancient bronze cooking vessel, symbolizes the spirit of Chinese culture.

Tourist Engagement:

Delve into the museum's expansive collection, which includes Chinese ceramics, paintings, calligraphy, sculptures, and artifacts from various dynasties. Engage with the exhibits through informative displays, multimedia presentations, and interactive elements. Don't miss the remarkable Jade Gallery, where intricate jade artifacts are showcased, and the Ancient Chinese Coin Gallery, displaying the evolution of currency.

Plan your visit during weekdays to avoid larger crowds, ensuring a more intimate and contemplative experience. The morning hours are generally quieter, providing an excellent opportunity to explore the exhibits at your own pace.

Consider participating in a guided tour for a deeper understanding of the artifacts and their cultural significance.

Website:
https://www.shanghaimuseum.net

Phone Number:
+86 21 6372 3500

Opening Hours:
9:00 AM to 5:00 PM, with the last admission at 4:00 PM.

ACROBATIC SHOWS AND THEATERS

Discover the captivating world of Chinese acrobatics, an ancient art form that seamlessly combines strength, agility, and grace. Shanghai has a rich tradition of hosting world-class acrobatic performances, showcasing the skills passed down through generations. While individual theaters may have unique histories, many share a commitment to preserving and evolving this incredible form of entertainment.

Prepare to be mesmerized by astonishing feats of flexibility, balance, and coordination. Acrobatic shows in Shanghai often feature breathtaking stunts, intricate choreography, and vibrant costumes. Audience participation is not uncommon, adding an interactive element to the performance.

Many theaters provide an immersive experience, allowing you to witness the precision and skill of the acrobats up close.

Evenings are the best time to experience acrobatic shows when the theaters come alive with dazzling lights and vibrant performances. Consider booking tickets in advance, especially during peak tourist seasons, to secure good seats. Arrive a bit early to soak in the atmosphere and enjoy any pre-show entertainment.

Websites:
http://www.shcircusworld.com/
http://www.shanghai-era.com/
http://www.shacrobaticshow.com/

Phone Numbers:
Shanghai Circus World: +86 21 6652 7755
ERA Intersection of Time: +86 21 6652 5468
Shanghai Acrobatic Troupe: +86 21 6372 5127

SHANGHAI DISNEY RESORT

Step into the magical world of Shanghai Disney Resort, a theme park that seamlessly blends Disney's enchanting storytelling with Chinese culture. Opened in June 2016, this resort is Disney's first in mainland China, featuring two main attractions: Disneyland Park and Disneytown. The park showcases Disney's commitment to creating immersive experiences for visitors of all ages.

Tourist Engagement:
Explore the wonders of Enchanted Storybook Castle, the largest and most interactive castle in any Disney theme park. Engage in thrilling rides, including TRON Lightcycle Power Run and Pirates of the Caribbean: Battle for the Sunken Treasure. Enjoy live performances, character meet-and-greets, and spectacular parades. Disneytown, the resort's shopping, dining, and entertainment district, offers a variety of experiences for visitors.

Weekdays, especially Tuesday through Thursday, tend to be less crowded than weekends. The off-season, typically during non-holiday weekdays in the spring and fall, offers a more relaxed experience.

WATERFRONT RETREATS AND PARKS

People's Square

Immerse yourself in the vibrant heart of Shanghai by visiting People's Square, a dynamic urban space that has witnessed the city's transformation. Originally a racetrack in the early 20th century, it underwent several changes and became People's Square in 1952. Today, it serves as a cultural, recreational, and transportation hub, surrounded by significant landmarks such as the Shanghai Museum and the Shanghai Grand Theatre.

Zhongshan Park

Experience a tranquil escape in the midst of bustling Shanghai by visiting Zhongshan Park, named after Sun Yat-sen, the founding father of modern China. Originally the Bubbling Well Cemetery in the early 20th century, it was later transformed into a beautiful public park. Today, Zhongshan Park offers a serene environment with lush greenery, scenic lakes, and a mix of traditional and modern features.

Century Park

Embark on a peaceful retreat within the bustling city by visiting Century Park, the largest park in Shanghai. Opened in 2000, this expansive green oasis was designed with a blend of traditional Chinese landscaping and modern features. Located in the Pudong New Area, Century Park offers a serene escape from the urban hustle, featuring lakes, gardens, and recreational spaces.

CULINARY ADVENTURES

Nanxiang Steamed Bun Restaurant

Nanxiang Steamed Bun Restaurant, located in the heart of Shanghai, holds a rich culinary history dating back to 1900. Renowned for its signature dish, the xiaolongbao (soup dumplings), this iconic establishment has become a symbol of Shanghai's culinary heritage. Originally situated in the old city of Nanxiang, the restaurant has expanded its legacy, maintaining its commitment to delivering authentic flavors.

Indulge in the artistry of Nanxiang's skilled chefs as they meticulously prepare xiaolongbao, delicate dumplings filled with flavorful broth and a variety of fillings. The restaurant offers a menu featuring a diverse selection of dim sum, dumplings, and traditional Shanghainese dishes. Besides the famous xiaolongbao, savor other regional specialties, such as shengjian bao (pan-fried dumplings) and savory noodles.

Nanxiang Steamed Bun Restaurant provides a cozy and traditional atmosphere, allowing diners to immerse themselves in the history and culture of Shanghai. The open kitchen concept allows you to observe the skilled chefs crafting each delicate dumpling. The restaurant's popularity among both locals and tourists adds a lively buzz to the dining experience.

Visit Nanxiang Steamed Bun Restaurant during off-peak hours to avoid long queues, especially during lunch and dinner rushes. Late mornings or early afternoons offer a more relaxed setting for a leisurely dim sum experience.

Address:
85 Yuyuan Road, Huangpu District, Shanghai, China
Phone Number:
+86 21 6355 4206

MUST TRY STREET FOOD IN CHENGHUANGMIAO

Shengjian Bao (Pan-Fried Soup Dumplings):

Chenghuangmiao is renowned for its exceptional shengjian bao, a local favorite that combines the best of both worlds – a crispy bottom, tender dough, and a flavorful filling bursting with juicy soup. These delectable pan-fried dumplings are often seasoned with sesame seeds and green onions, creating a symphony of flavors with each bite.

Jianbing (Savory Crepes):

Experience the magic of jianbing, a popular street breakfast that has captivated both locals and visitors alike. Thin crepes are skillfully spread with a savory mixture of eggs, sauces, fresh herbs, and crispy wonton crackers. Folded into a convenient wrap, jianbing is the epitome of a satisfying and convenient street snack.

Tanghulu (Candied Fruits on Skewers):

Indulge your sweet cravings with tanghulu, a delightful treat that transforms ordinary fruits into sugary delights. Skewered fruits, often strawberries or hawthorns, are coated in a glossy layer of hardened sugar, creating a crunchy shell around the succulent fruit.

Xiaolongbao (Soup Dumplings):

No culinary exploration in Chenghuangmiao is complete without savoring the iconic xiaolongbao. These delicate steamed dumplings encapsulate a flavorful broth along with a variety of fillings, typically pork or crab. The artistry lies in the thinness of the dumpling skin, ensuring a perfect balance between the tender casing and the savory contents.

Niangao (Sticky Rice Cake):

Experience the comforting warmth of niangao, a traditional Chinese New Year treat available year-round in Chenghuangmiao. These sticky rice cakes come in various flavors such as red bean or osmanthus, providing a chewy and satisfying snack. The subtle sweetness and unique textures make niangao a delightful option for those with a penchant for traditional desserts.

Michelin-starred Restaurants

Ultraviolet by Paul Pairet (3 Michelin Stars):

At the pinnacle of Shanghai's culinary excellence is Ultraviolet, an avant-garde dining venture by acclaimed chef Paul Pairet. With three Michelin stars, Ultraviolet transcends traditional dining by seamlessly integrating multisensory elements. Limited to only ten guests per seating, the immersive journey combines cutting-edge technology, artful presentation, and meticulously crafted dishes, offering an unparalleled gastronomic spectacle.

T'ang Court (3 Michelin Stars):

T'ang Court, nestled in The Langham, Xintiandi, boasts three Michelin stars for its exquisite Cantonese cuisine. Led by Chef Justin Tan, the restaurant delivers a harmonious blend of traditional and contemporary flavors. Signature dishes such as the Baked Abalone Puff with Diced Chicken and the Double-Boiled Fish Maw Soup exemplify the culinary mastery that earned T'ang Court its prestigious accolades.

Jade on 36 (1 Michelin Star):

Perched atop the Pudong Shangri-La, Jade on 36 enchants diners with breathtaking views of the city skyline along with its Michelin-starred cuisine. With a focus on modern European dishes, Chef Paul Eschbach crafts a menu that reflects both innovation and elegance. From delectable seafood creations to meticulously prepared meats, Jade on 36 offers a sophisticated dining experience that lingers in the memory.

8 1/2 Otto e Mezzo Bombana (3 Michelin Stars):

Heralded as a culinary gem in Shanghai's vibrant dining scene, 8 1/2 Otto e Mezzo Bombana, with its three Michelin stars, presents an indulgent journey into Italian gastronomy. Renowned Chef Umberto Bombana curates a menu where every dish is an artistic expression of premium ingredients and culinary finesse. From homemade pasta to succulent meats, each creation is a testament to the restaurant's commitment to culinary excellence.

Night Food Markets

Nanshi Night Market:

Nestled in the historic Old City, Nanshi Night Market is a sensory delight that immerses visitors in traditional Shanghainese flavors. From aromatic stews and skewered delicacies to the famous xiaolongbao, this market showcases the rich tapestry of local cuisine. The vibrant atmosphere, with neon lights and bustling crowds, adds an extra layer of excitement to the culinary journey.

Jing'an Night Market:

Situated in the trendy Jing'an district, this night market caters to both locals and expats with its diverse selection of international and local cuisines. From sizzling Korean barbecue to authentic Sichuan hot pot, Jing'an Night Market is a melting pot of flavors. The modern setting, coupled with live music and cultural performances, elevates the dining experience.

Zhongshan Park Night Market:

Bringing a lively atmosphere to the Zhongshan Park area, this night market is a favorite among locals for its eclectic mix of street food.

Yuyuan Bazaar:

Adjacent to the iconic Yuyuan Garden, Yuyuan Bazaar transforms into a bustling night market as dusk falls. The market's narrow lanes are lined with stalls offering an array of street food, from spicy hot pots to crispy scallion pancakes. The ambiance is heightened by traditional Chinese architecture and the glow of lanterns, creating a charming backdrop for an evening culinary exploration.

Xiangyang Road Night Market:

Xiangyang Road Night Market, located in the heart of the Former French Concession, is a culinary haven that opens its stalls as the sun sets. This market seamlessly blends international influences with local Shanghai tastes. Visitors can sample everything from Taiwanese bubble tea to French pastries, creating a fusion of global flavors.

From grilled skewers and seafood delights to sweet treats like cotton candy and bubble waffles, Zhongshan Park Night Market offers a diverse culinary journey under the glittering night sky.

CLASSIC SHANGHAI IN 3 DAYS

Day 1: The Bund and Pudong

Morning:
Breakfast at a local café: $10
Explore The Bund, a historic waterfront area: Free

Afternoon:
Lunch at a riverside restaurant: $20
Visit the Shanghai Museum: $15
Stroll along The Bund for iconic skyline views: Free

Evening:
Dinner at a Pudong restaurant with a view: $30
Explore Pudong's Lujiazui area: Free

Day 2: Yuyuan Garden and Old Town

Morning:
Breakfast at a local teahouse: $15
Explore Yuyuan Garden: $10
Visit Yuyuan Bazaar for souvenirs: $20

Afternoon:
Lunch at a traditional Shanghainese restaurant: $25
Wander through the Old Town: Free
Visit City God Temple: $5

Evening:
Dinner at a local street food market: $15
Optional: Attend a traditional Chinese acrobatic show: $40.

Day 3: French Concession and Art Districts

Morning:
Breakfast at a French-style bakery: $12
Explore the Former French Concession: Free
Visit Fuxing Park: Free

Afternoon:
Lunch at a local bistro: $30
Explore Tianzifang Art District: Free
Visit M50 Art District: Free

Evening:
Dinner at a trendy French Concession restaurant: $35
Enjoy nightlife in Xinle Road: Budget for drinks: $207

Estimated Total Expenses (excluding accommodation): $475

The Bund in Shanghai, with its blend of colonial architecture and modern skyscrapers, offers a glimpse into the city's rich history. Across the Huangpu River, Pudong's futuristic skyline showcases Shanghai's rapid evolution. This dynamic contrast makes the Bund and Pudong essential stops for experiencing Shanghai's vibrant urban landscape.

Yu Garden and the Old Town in Shanghai transport visitors to ancient China. Yu Garden, with its intricate design and serene ponds, offers a peaceful escape from the bustling city. The nearby Old Town features traditional architecture, winding alleys, and vibrant markets, providing a glimpse into Shanghai's rich cultural heritage.

Exploring the French Concession in Shanghai unveils tree-lined streets, elegant villas, and charming cafes, echoing its European influence. Nearby art districts like Tianzifang and M50 boast vibrant galleries and boutiques, showcasing the city's contemporary creativity. Together, they offer a captivating blend of history, culture, and artistic expression.

FAMILY-FRIENDLY EXPLORATION

Day 1: Shanghai Disney Resort

Morning:
Start your day with a magical breakfast at one of the resort's themed restaurants: $20
Head to Shanghai Disneyland Park: Full-day admission ticket: $70

Afternoon:
Lunch in the park at a Disney-themed eatery: $25
Explore Fantasyland, Adventure Isle, and Tomorrowland: Free
Catch the afternoon parade and live shows: Free

Evening:
Dinner at Disneytown: $30
Enjoy the evening spectacular, "Ignite the Dream": Free
Optional: Explore the nightlife at Disneytown: Budget for drinks: $20

Day 1 Estimated Expenses: $165

Day 2: Science and Technology Museums

Morning:
Breakfast at a local café near your accommodation: $10
Visit the China Science and Technology Museum: Admission fee: $15

Afternoon:
Lunch at a nearby restaurant: $20
Explore the Beijing Planetarium: Admission fee: $10
Visit the National Museum of China (Science and Technology Hall): Free

Evening:
Dinner at a restaurant in the area: $25
Relax at a nearby park or stroll around the Olympic Green: Free

Day 2 Estimated Expenses: $80

Day 3: Family Parks and Entertainment

Morning:
Enjoy breakfast at a family-friendly café: $15
Head to Happy Valley Beijing: Full-day admission ticket: $40

Afternoon:
Lunch inside the amusement park: $20
Explore various themed zones and enjoy rides: Free
Attend live performances and shows: Free

Evening:
Dinner at the park or nearby dining options: $25
Relax in the evening at a local family park or entertainment area: Free

Day 3 Estimated Expenses: $100

Overall Estimated Expenses for the Trip: $345

Shanghai Disney Resort promises enchantment with its iconic castle, thrilling rides, and beloved characters, captivating visitors of all ages. From the magical wonder of Fantasyland to the futuristic charm of Tomorrowland, the resort offers a unique blend of Disney magic and Chinese culture, creating unforgettable memories for guests.

Shanghai's Science and Technology Museums offer an immersive journey into innovation and discovery. From interactive exhibits exploring space and robotics to hands-on experiments showcasing cutting-edge technology, visitors delve into the wonders of science. These museums inspire curiosity, education, and appreciation for the advancements shaping our world.

Shanghai's family parks and entertainment venues offer endless fun for all ages. From the thrilling rides at Happy Valley to the whimsical attractions at Shanghai Zoo, there's something for everyone. Families can bond over exciting adventures, live performances, and immersive experiences, creating cherished memories in the heart of the city.

ARTS AND CULTURE ITINERARY

Day 1: M50 Art District

Morning:
Breakfast at a local cafe near M50: $10
Explore contemporary art at M50 Art District: Free

Afternoon:
Lunch at a trendy M50 restaurant: $20
Dive into art galleries and studios: Free
Enjoy a coffee break at a M50 cafe: $5

Evening:
Dinner at a nearby restaurant: $25
Optional: Attend an art event or exhibition in the evening: Ticket prices may vary

Day 1 Estimated Expenses: $60 (excluding optional event)

Day 2: Shanghai Museum and Theaters

Morning:
Breakfast at your accommodation or a nearby cafe: $10
Visit the Shanghai Museum: Admission fee: $15

Afternoon:
Lunch at a restaurant near the museum: $20
Explore People's Square and enjoy the urban surroundings: Free
Attend a matinee performance at a local theater: Ticket prices may vary

Evening:
Dinner at a restaurant in the theater district: $30
Stroll around Nanjing Road for evening shopping: Free

Day 2 Estimated Expenses: $75 (excluding theater ticket)

Day 3: Literary Cafes and Bookstores

Morning:
Breakfast at a literary-themed cafe: $15
Visit a local bookstore or explore the Book City: Free

Afternoon:
Lunch at a bookstore cafe: $20
Attend a book reading or literary event if available: Free or ticket prices may vary
Spend the afternoon reading and relaxing: Free

Evening:
Dinner at a cozy literary-themed restaurant: $25
Explore a local neighborhood for evening ambiance: Free

Day 3 Estimated Expenses: $60 (excluding optional literary event)

Overall Estimated Expenses for the Trip: $195

M50 Art District in Shanghai is a vibrant hub of contemporary creativity. Former industrial warehouses now house galleries, studios, and avant-garde exhibitions, showcasing the cutting-edge of Chinese and international art. Visitors immerse themselves in a dynamic fusion of traditional and modern artistic expressions, making M50 a must-visit destination for art enthusiasts.

Shanghai Museum houses a vast collection of ancient Chinese art and artifacts, offering insights into the country's rich cultural heritage. Meanwhile, theaters like Shanghai Grand Theatre host world-class performances, from ballet to opera, captivating audiences with their artistic excellence. Together, they offer a captivating blend of history, culture, and entertainment.

Shanghai's literary cafes and bookstores offer a cozy retreat for book lovers and intellectuals alike. From the historic charm of Old China Hand Reading Room to the trendy ambiance of Page One Café, visitors can immerse themselves in literature while savoring artisanal coffee and engaging in stimulating conversations.

NATURE AND RELAXATION ESCAPE

Day 1: Zhongshan Park

Morning:
Breakfast at a local teahouse near Zhongshan Park: $15
Explore Zhongshan Park and enjoy a morning stroll: Free

Afternoon:
Lunch at a nearby restaurant: $20
Visit the Monument to the People's Heroes: Free
Explore the Military Museum of the Chinese People's Revolution: Admission fee: $10

Evening:
Dinner at a restaurant near Zhongshan Park: $25
Optional: Attend a local cultural event or performance: Ticket prices may vary

Day 1 Estimated Expenses: $70 (excluding optional event)

Day 2: Suzhou Creek and Waterfront

Morning:
Breakfast at a riverside café: $15
Stroll along Suzhou Creek and enjoy the waterfront views: Free

Afternoon:
Lunch at a waterfront restaurant: $25
Explore the North Bund area: Free
Take a boat tour along Suzhou Creek: $30

Evening:
Dinner at a restaurant with a view: $35
Relax at a waterfront park or plaza: Free

Day 2 Estimated Expenses: $105

Day 1: Street Food Safari

Morning:
Breakfast at a local street food market: $10
Explore Wangfujing Snack Street for morning bites: Free

Afternoon:
Lunch at a street food market or vendor: $15
Visit Houhai Hutong area for more street food delights: Free
Enjoy a tea or dessert break at a local teahouse: $10

Evening:
Dinner at a lively night market (e.g., Donghuamen Night Market): $20
Stroll around Nanluoguxiang for evening snacks: Free

Day 1 Estimated Expenses: $55

Overall Estimated Expenses for the Trip: $230

Zhongshan Park in Shanghai offers a tranquil oasis amidst the bustling cityscape. Visitors can stroll through lush gardens, admire scenic lakes, and enjoy recreational activities like boating and picnicking. With its historical monuments, serene ambiance, and vibrant flora, Zhongshan Park provides a refreshing escape for locals and tourists alike.

Suzhou Creek and its waterfront in Shanghai offer a captivating blend of history and modernity. Strolling along its banks, visitors can admire the juxtaposition of old warehouses and sleek skyscrapers, while soaking in the scenic views of the city skyline. The creek's revitalized waterfront promenade provides a serene escape amidst urban bustle.

Embarking on a street food safari in Shanghai is a culinary adventure not to be missed. From bustling night markets to hidden alleyway stalls, visitors can savor a tantalizing array of local delicacies, from xiaolongbao to scallion pancakes, experiencing the vibrant flavors and diverse culinary traditions of the city.

HIDDEN GEMS AND LOCAL FAVORITES

Secret Cafes and Hangouts

Seesaw Coffee: Nestled in the heart of the Former French Concession, Seesaw Coffee is an elusive spot favored by locals in the know. Behind a discreet entrance, patrons discover a minimalist oasis with exposed brick walls and ample natural light. The carefully crafted coffee and artisanal pastries make Seesaw a haven for coffee enthusiasts seeking a tranquil escape.

Lost Bakery: Concealed in the labyrinthine lanes of Tianzifang, Lost Bakery is a quaint space exuding rustic charm. Beyond its unassuming facade lies a cozy retreat with vintage decor and a charming courtyard. The aroma of freshly baked goods wafts through the air, creating an irresistible allure for those in search of a hidden haven.

Sumerian Coffee: Tucked away in a nondescript building in Jing'an, Sumerian Coffee remains a well-guarded secret among locals. This micro-roastery combines a love for specialty coffee with an intimate setting. The industrial-chic ambiance and expertly brewed coffee create an atmosphere where patrons can savor the art of coffee-making in seclusion.

Egg: Hiding in plain sight within the vibrant Xintiandi area, Egg is a unique cafe blending vintage aesthetics with contemporary design. Behind its unpretentious facade lies a treasure trove of carefully curated art and literature. The menu, featuring inventive egg-based dishes, adds to the allure, making Egg a clandestine spot for cultural indulgence.

Fu He Hui: Disguised as an ordinary villa in the Jing'an district, Fu He Hui is a hidden vegetarian gem. Beyond its unremarkable exterior lies a Michelin-starred restaurant offering a plant-based culinary journey. The serene atmosphere and meticulously crafted dishes make Fu He Hui a secret retreat for those seeking gastronomic excellence.

Offbeat Art Galleries

HOW Art Museum: Nestled in the heart of Pudong, the HOW Art Museum stands as an architectural marvel, resembling a giant metallic coil. Beyond its striking exterior lies a space dedicated to cutting-edge contemporary art. HOW seamlessly blends exhibitions, installations, and immersive experiences, inviting visitors into a world where imagination knows no limits.

ART LABOR Gallery: Housed in a former slaughterhouse in the Moganshan Art District, ART LABOR Gallery is a quirky haven for unconventional art. This gallery thrives on showcasing experimental and boundary-pushing works by both local and international artists. Its raw, industrial setting complements the boldness of the exhibited pieces, creating an immersive experience that challenges the conventional gallery aesthetic.

Leo Xu Projects: Tucked away in the leafy French Concession, Leo Xu Projects is a contemporary art space known for its commitment to emerging talents. The gallery, founded by curator Leo Xu, defies traditional norms by fostering a dynamic environment for artistic experimentation. It provides a

Chronus Art Center: Situated in the thriving art scene of West Bund, the Chronus Art Center focuses on the intersection of art, science, and technology. This experimental space hosts exhibitions that delve into the realms of new media and digital art. The center's commitment to fostering interdisciplinary collaborations results in thought-provoking installations and interactive experiences that redefine the boundaries of artistic expression.

Authentic Local Eateries

Jia Jia Tang Bao: Nestled in the heart of the city, Jia Jia Tang Bao is a celebrated eatery renowned for its exceptional xiaolongbao, or soup dumplings. The delicate, handcrafted dumplings burst with savory broth and succulent pork, creating a symphony of flavors in every bite. The no-frills ambiance and the artistry of their chefs make it a must-visit for those craving an authentic taste of Shanghai's culinary heritage.
Located near People's Square metro station. Exit the station and walk south on Huanghe Rd. Jia Jia Tang Bao will be on your left.

Old Jesse: For a journey into Shanghainese comfort food, Old Jesse is an iconic restaurant that captures the essence of local cuisine. Known for its braised dishes and homely atmosphere, this eatery serves up classics like Red Cooked Pork and Lion's Head Meatballs. The ambiance exudes a nostalgic charm, making diners feel as if they've stepped into a traditional Shanghainese home.

Yang's Fry Dumplings: A visit to Shanghai wouldn't be complete without savoring the crispy-bottomed, pan-fried goodness of Sheng Jian Bao at Yang's Fry Dumplings. These succulent pork-filled dumplings boast a unique combination of textures, with a crispy base giving way to a juicy and flavorful interior. The simplicity of the menu and the bustling atmosphere make it a beloved spot for locals and tourists alike. Close to Nanjing East Road metro station. Exit the station and walk south on Huanghe Rd. Yang's Fry Dumplings will be on your left.

Da Hu Chun: Da Hu Chun, renowned for its pan-fried pork buns, elevates the humble street food experience to a gastronomic delight. The handcrafted buns feature a crispy exterior and juicy filling, delivering a satisfying crunch with each bite. The eatery's commitment to quality and consistency has earned it a dedicated following among food enthusiasts seeking an authentic taste of Shanghai's culinary heritage.
Near Yuyuan Garden metro station. Exit the station and walk west on Fuyou Rd. Da Hu Chun is located on the left side.

Non-touristy Souvenir Shops

Market : Nestled in the heart of the city, Dongtai Road Antique Market offers a curated collection of vintage items, antiques, and collectibles. It's a treasure trove for those seeking distinctive souvenirs such as traditional Chinese artifacts, retro posters, and handcrafted trinkets. The market exudes an authentic charm and provides a unique shopping experience away from mainstream tourist hubs.
Take Line 10 to Yuyuan Garden station. Exit the station and walk south on Fuyou Rd, then turn right onto Dongtai Rd. Dongtai Road Antique Market will be on your left.

Tianzifang: While Tianzifang is a popular destination, certain corners of this labyrinthine arts and crafts enclave offer non-commercialized treasures. Away from the main thoroughfares, you'll discover boutique shops showcasing locally-made art, ceramics, and textiles. These hidden gems provide an opportunity to support local artists and artisans while acquiring one-of-a-kind souvenirs.

Sinan Mansions : Sinan Mansions, a historical area reimagined into a contemporary lifestyle hub, houses boutique shops that showcase a fusion of modern and traditional craftsmanship. Here, you can find unique items like handcrafted jewelry, designer homeware, and bespoke fashion pieces, offering an elevated and non-touristy shopping experience.
Near Xintiandi metro station. Exit the station and walk south on Madang Rd, then turn left onto Sinan Rd. Sinan Mansions will be on your right.

South Bund Fabric Market : For those with an appreciation for bespoke tailoring and textiles, the South Bund Fabric Market is an ideal destination. Amidst the myriad fabric stalls, you'll find skilled tailors who can craft custom-made clothing. This market provides a personal touch to your souvenirs, allowing you to take home a piece of Shanghai tailored to your preferences.
Take Line 4 to Luban Road station. Exit the station and walk east on Luban Rd, then turn right onto Lujiabang Rd. South Bund Fabric Market is located on your left.

NIGHTLIFE AND ENTERTAINME

Rooftop Bars with a View

Flair Rooftop, The Ritz-Carlton Shanghai, Pudong: Perched atop The Ritz-Carlton in Pudong, Flair Rooftop stands as an epitome of sophistication and luxury. With an expansive terrace boasting unobstructed views of the Oriental Pearl Tower and the futuristic Pudong skyline, it offers a glamorous setting for cocktails and socializing. The chic ambiance, coupled with an extensive drink menu and attentive service, makes Flair Rooftop a must-visit for those seeking a refined and panoramic experience.
Address: 8 Century Avenue, Lujiazui, Pudong, Shanghai, China.

CHAR Bar & Grill, Hotel Indigo Shanghai on the Bund: Nestled along the historic Bund, CHAR Bar & Grill at Hotel Indigo presents a stylish rooftop escape. The terrace provides a front-row seat to the historic architecture of the Bund on one side and the modern skyscrapers of Pudong on the other. This dual perspective encapsulates the essence of Shanghai's architectural evolution. The menu features an array of signature cocktails and delectable bites, creating a perfect blend of ambiance and gastronomy.
Address: 585 Zhongshan East 2nd Rd, Hongkou District, Shanghai, China.

Barbarossa, People's Park: Set against the backdrop of lush greenery in People's Park, Barbarossa offers a unique rooftop experience with a blend of old and new Shanghai. Housed in a renovated colonial building, the terrace overlooks the city's skyline and the tranquil park below. The atmosphere is infused with a Middle Eastern vibe, creating an exotic ambiance. Barbarossa is renowned for its cocktails, shisha offerings, and a distinctive rooftop setting that transports visitors to a different era.
Address: 231 Nanjing West Rd, Huangpu District, Shanghai, China.

Trendy Nightclubs

MINT: Situated in the heart of the city, MINT is synonymous with opulence and exclusivity. Boasting a sleek and futuristic design, this iconic nightclub offers breathtaking views of the Shanghai skyline from its terrace. MINT attracts an upscale crowd with its high-energy atmosphere, resident DJs spinning top-notch beats, and an extensive list of premium cocktails. The combination of avant-garde aesthetics and a pulsating dance floor makes MINT a hotspot for those seeking a glamorous and trendy nightlife experience.
Address: 318 Fuzhou Rd, Hongkou District, Shanghai, China.

Le Baron: Tucked away in a historic building on the Bund, Le Baron is a renowned nightclub that exudes a chic and eclectic vibe. Known for its cutting-edge music programming featuring international DJs and an intimate dance floor, Le Baron attracts a diverse and fashionable crowd. The venue's art-inspired interiors and ever-evolving theme nights contribute to its reputation as one of Shanghai's trendiest nightclubs.
Address: 7F, 20 Donghu Rd, Xuhui District, Shanghai, China.

Arkham: For lovers of electronic music and underground vibes, Arkham stands as a mecca in Shanghai's nightclub scene. Situated in the French Concession, this edgy venue hosts a range of events from techno and house to experimental sounds. With its gritty industrial aesthetic, Arkham appeals to a diverse crowd of music enthusiasts seeking an alternative and trendsetting club experience.
Address: 1 Wulumuqi Rd, Jing'an District, Shanghai, China.

Bar Rouge: Perched atop Bund 18 with a commanding view of the iconic skyline, Bar Rouge is a glamorous nightclub that seamlessly combines sophistication with a lively atmosphere. Known for its themed parties, celebrity appearances, and resident DJs, Bar Rouge has been a staple in Shanghai's nightlife for over a decade. The chic decor, creative cocktails, and a dance floor that comes alive after dark make it a trendy destination for those looking to see and be seen.
Address: 18 Zhongshan East 1st Rd, Huangpu District, Shanghai, China.

Traditional Teahouses

Huxinting Tea House : Nestled in the heart of the Yuyuan Garden, Huxinting Tea House is a venerable establishment with a history dating back to the Ming Dynasty. Its iconic location, surrounded by picturesque ponds and classical Chinese architecture, creates a serene ambiance. Patrons can indulge in a diverse selection of teas, accompanied by delicate dim sum. The traditional tea ceremony performances further enhance the cultural immersion, making Huxinting a haven for tea enthusiasts seeking an authentic experience.
Address: 257 Yuyuan Rd, Huangpu District, Shanghai, China.
Directions: Near Yuyuan Garden metro station. Exit the station and walk west on Fuyou Rd, then turn left onto Yuyuan Rd. Huxinting Tea House is located within Yuyuan Garden.

Song Fang Maison de Thé : Located in the historic French Concession, Song Fang Maison de Thé is a contemporary teahouse that beautifully blends tradition with modernity. The serene and minimalist decor provides a tranquil setting for tea appreciation. With a focus on high-quality, hand-selected teas, Song Fang Maison de Thé offers an educational journey into the world of Chinese tea, complete with knowledgeable staff guiding guests through the nuances of each brew.
Address: 5 Sinan Rd, Luwan District, Shanghai, China.
Directions: Close to Dapuqiao metro station. Exit the station and walk south on Madang Rd, then turn left onto Sinan Rd. Song Fang Maison de Thé is located on your right.

Tianshan Tea City : For those looking to explore a myriad of tea varieties, Tianshan Tea City stands as a comprehensive destination in Shanghai. This multi-level complex houses numerous tea stalls, each specializing in distinct types of tea. From fragrant green teas to robust oolongs, visitors can sample and purchase a diverse range of leaves. Tianshan Tea City provides a vibrant and bustling environment, offering a unique opportunity to immerse oneself in China's rich tea heritage.
Address: 518 Zhongshan West Rd, Changning District, Shanghai, China. **Directions**: Near Jiangsu Road metro station. Exit the station and walk west on Zhongshan West Rd.

Night Markets and Events

Nanjing Road Pedestrian Street: Nanjing Road, one of Shanghai's most iconic shopping streets, transforms into a lively pedestrian area by night. The bustling atmosphere is accentuated by vibrant street performances, dazzling neon lights, and a myriad of street vendors selling everything from local snacks to souvenirs. It's a perfect blend of shopping, entertainment, and the vibrant pulse of the city.
Address: Nanjing Rd, Huangpu District, Shanghai, China.
Directions: Close to East Nanjing Road metro station. Exit the station and walk east on Nanjing Rd. Nanjing Road Pedestrian Street stretches between People's Square and the Bund.

Yuyuan Bazaar: Adjacent to the historic Yuyuan Garden, the Yuyuan Bazaar is a night market that immerses visitors in traditional Chinese architecture and culture. The market's narrow alleys are lined with stalls offering a plethora of goods, including handicrafts, antiques, and local snacks. As you wander through the labyrinthine lanes, the blend of historical charm and modern commerce creates an enchanting experience.
Address: 269 Fangbang Middle Rd, Huangpu District, Shanghai, China.
Directions: Near Yuyuan Garden metro station. Exit the station and walk west on Fuyou Rd, then turn right onto Fangbang Middle Rd. Yuyuan Bazaar is located near Yuyuan Garden.

Jiashan Market: Jiashan Market is a dynamic weekend event that showcases the creative and artisanal side of Shanghai. Held in the atmospheric Jiashan Road neighborhood, the market features an eclectic mix of handmade crafts, vintage finds, and gourmet treats. Live music performances and art installations contribute to the vibrant and bohemian atmosphere, making it a must-visit for those seeking unique, locally-crafted treasures.
Address: 259 Jiashan Rd, Xuhui District, Shanghai, China.
Directions: Close to Jiashan Road metro station. Exit the station and walk south on Jiashan Rd. Jiashan Market is located on the left side of the road.

SHOPPING IN SHANGHAI

Luxury Shopping Districts

Huaihai Road : Regarded as one of Shanghai's premier shopping streets, Huaihai Road is synonymous with luxury and sophistication. This bustling avenue, flanked by lush trees and historical architecture, houses an impressive lineup of designer boutiques, flagship stores, and international luxury brands. From iconic fashion houses to haute couture labels, Huaihai Road is a haven for those seeking the epitome of upscale shopping in Shanghai.

Directions: Huaihai Road is a major thoroughfare in Shanghai that spans across several districts, including Huangpu, Xuhui, and Jing'an. It runs east-west and is easily accessible by various metro stations along the route.

Nanjing Road West: Situated in the heart of the city, Nanjing Road West is a renowned luxury shopping destination that rivals the world's most prestigious retail districts. This upscale thoroughfare is home to an array of high-end department stores, including the historic Shanghai No.1 Department Store and the lavish Plaza 66. With a dazzling display of international and Chinese luxury brands, Nanjing Road West offers a glamorous shopping experience amid the city's iconic skyline.

Directions: Nanjing Road West is located in the Jing'an District of Shanghai. Visitors can take the metro to West Nanjing Road station (Lines 2, 12, and 13) and walk east along Nanjing Road West. The luxury shopping district extends from Jing'an Temple towards People's Square.

Xintiandi: Xintiandi, an upscale lifestyle and entertainment district, seamlessly blends historic Shikumen architecture with modern sophistication. This pedestrian-friendly enclave is dotted with luxury boutiques, designer flagship stores, and upscale international brands. The chic ambiance, coupled with a diverse range of fine dining options, makes Xintiandi a magnet for those seeking a curated and refined shopping experience in a culturally rich setting.

Antique and Vintage Finds

Liuhe Road Antique Market:
Liuhe Road Antique Market, located near Fuxing Park, is another gem for those seeking vintage finds. This market specializes in Chinese and Asian antiques, including calligraphy, porcelain, and traditional art pieces. The knowledgeable sellers and the eclectic mix of items create an immersive experience for collectors and enthusiasts alike. The market is particularly known for its authenticity and variety of artifacts spanning different dynasties.
Directions: Take Line 10 to Yuyuan Garden station. Exit the station and walk south on Fuyou Rd, then turn left onto Liuhe Rd. Liuhe Road Antique Market is located on your right.

South Bund Soft-Spinning Material Market: While primarily known for fabrics, the South Bund Soft-Spinning Material Market is a hidden treasure for vintage fashion enthusiasts. Amidst the textile vendors, there are stalls offering vintage clothing, accessories, and retro-inspired pieces. Bargaining is part of the experience, and visitors can uncover unique fashion finds from different eras. The market provides a distinctive blend of old and new within a vibrant setting.
Directions: Take Line 4 to Luban Road station. Exit the station and walk east on Luban Rd, then turn right onto Lujiabang Rd. South Bund Soft-Spinning Material Market is located on your left.

Shanghai Antique Furniture Mart : For those in search of antique furniture and home decor, the Shanghai Antique Furniture Mart is a dedicated marketplace. Situated in the Hongqiao area, this expansive market showcases a vast selection of Ming and Qing Dynasty furniture, intricately carved screens, and antique home accessories. The authenticity of the pieces and the knowledgeable vendors make it a go-to destina
Directions: Take Line 7 to Changping Road station. Exit the station and walk south on Changping Rd, then turn right onto Kangding Rd. Shanghai Antique Furniture Mart is located on your right.

Local Designers and Boutiques

Mary Ching: Founded by Jenny Kam, Mary Ching is a luxury footwear brand that seamlessly blends Chinese heritage with modern design. Specializing in elegant and intricately crafted shoes, Mary Ching's creations often feature traditional Chinese silk brocade, embroidery, and other cultural elements. The boutique, located in the heart of the French Concession, serves as a showcase for the brand's exquisite footwear, reflecting a harmonious marriage of East and West.
Directions: Close to Yuyuan Garden metro station. Exit the station and walk west on Fuyou Rd, then turn right onto Yuyuan Rd. Mary Ching is located on your left.

Fake Natoo: Fake Natoo, founded by Zhou Na, is a contemporary fashion label that embraces sustainable and ethical practices. Known for its minimalist aesthetic and clean lines, the brand offers a range of versatile clothing, often made from eco-friendly materials. The boutique, situated in the trendy Tianzifang area, attracts fashion enthusiasts seeking stylish pieces with a conscience, emphasizing both design and sustainability.
Directions: Close to Jiaotong University metro station. Exit the station and walk south on Huashan Rd. Fake Natoo is located on the left side of the road.

Decoster Concept Store: Curated by fashion influencer Nicole Zhang, Decoster Concept Store is a boutique that celebrates emerging Chinese designers. Located in the West Bund area, this concept store showcases a carefully curated selection of clothing, accessories, and lifestyle items. The space serves as a platform for local talent, providing a unique shopping experience for those looking to discover cutting-edge fashion in Shanghai.
Directions: Close to Huangpi South Road metro station. Exit the station and walk west on Huaihai Middle Rd. Decoster Concept Store is located on your right.

Bargain Markets

Qipu Road Clothing Market:
Nestled in the heart of the city, Qipu Road Clothing Market is a bustling labyrinth of narrow alleys lined with stalls and shops offering a vast selection of affordable clothing. Renowned as one of the largest wholesale markets in Shanghai, Qipu Road is a haven for bargain hunters looking for trendy fashion pieces, accessories, and textiles. The market is known for its rock-bottom prices, particularly for bulk purchases, and provides a vibrant and dynamic shopping experience.

Directions: Take Line 10 to Qipu Road station. Exit the station and walk north on Qipu Rd. Qipu Road Clothing Market is located along both sides of the road.

AP Plaza (Xinyang Fashion and Gifts Market): Situated near the Science and Technology Museum metro station, AP Plaza is a popular destination for those seeking knock-off designer goods, electronics, and accessories. The market is home to numerous stalls offering a diverse range of products, from bags and clothing to watches and gadgets. Bargaining is a key element of the shopping experience at AP Plaza, allowing visitors to secure deals on a variety of items. While the market is known for its imitation products, it's essential for buyers to exercise discernment.

Directions: Take Line 2 to Century Avenue station. Exit the station and walk east on Century Ave. AP Plaza (Xinyang Fashion and Gifts Market) is located in the Global Harbor shopping mall.

Hongqiao New World Pearl Market: For those interested in jewelry, pearls, and accessories, the Hongqiao New World Pearl Market is a treasure trove of affordable finds. Located near Hongqiao Railway Station, this market specializes in pearls, gemstones, and traditional Chinese jewelry. Shoppers can browse through a vast selection of necklaces, earrings, and bracelets, with the option to customize pieces. The market's competitive prices and the opportunity to haggle make it a go-to destination for those looking to add some sparkle to their collection without breaking the bank.

Directions: Take Line 10 to Shuicheng Road station. Exit the station and walk south on Hongmei Rd.

ACCOMMODATION RECOMMENDATS

Luxury Hotels with a View

The Ritz-Carlton Shanghai, Pudong:

Perched on the upper floors of a skyscraper in the heart of Lujiazui, The Ritz-Carlton Shanghai, Pudong offers unparalleled views of the iconic Oriental Pearl Tower and the Huangpu River. The luxurious accommodations, paired with world-class service, make it a haven for discerning travelers. Dining options such as Jin Xuan for fine Chinese cuisine and Aura for rooftop cocktails add to the allure of this prestigious hotel.

Location: Lujiazui, Pudong
Phone Number: +86 21 2020 1111

The Peninsula Shanghai:

Nestled along the historic Bund, The Peninsula Shanghai is an epitome of elegance and sophistication. The hotel's Art Deco architecture provides a nod to Shanghai's past, while its rooms and suites offer panoramic views of the Huangpu River and Pudong skyline. The Peninsula's rooftop terrace, Sir Elly's Terrace, is a perfect vantage point to enjoy the breathtaking scenery.

Location: The Bund
Phone Number: +86 21 2327 2888

Fairmont Peace Hotel:

Situated on the historic Bund, the Fairmont Peace Hotel seamlessly blends classic and contemporary elements. This iconic hotel, with its Jazz Age heritage, presents stunning views of the Huangpu River and Pudong's glittering skyline. The opulent accommodations, coupled with the hotel's rich history, create a timeless atmosphere for guests seeking luxury with a touch of nostalgia.

Location: The Bund
Phone Number: +86 21 6138 6888

Luxury hotel expenses in Shanghai can vary widely based on room category, time of booking, and seasonal factors. Generally, nightly rates for these top-tier hotels start from approximately $300 to $800 or more, depending on the room type and specific details of the stay. It's recommended to check the hotel websites or contact them directly for the most accurate and up-to-date pricing information.

The Ritz-Carlton Shanghai, Pudong offers stunning city skyline views and luxurious amenities like a spa and indoor pool. Its prime location in Pudong's financial district is convenient for exploring attractions. However, it's pricey, with limited local dining options nearby, and can feel crowded at times.

The Peninsula Shanghai boasts historic charm and impeccable service in an Art Deco setting. Its prime Bund location offers easy access to landmarks. However, it's pricey and may not offer consistent views. Surroundings can get crowded due to its popularity among tourists.

The Fairmont Peace Hotel is a historic landmark with an elegant Art Deco ambiance along the Bund. Its convenient location offers access to scenic promenades and upscale amenities. However, aging infrastructure and pricey dining options may deter some guests seeking modern comforts and affordability.

Boutique Stays in French Concession

The Middle House:

Situated in the heart of the French Concession, The Middle House is a stylish and contemporary boutique hotel that seamlessly blends modern luxury with traditional Chinese elements. The rooms and suites, adorned with elegant furnishings, provide a serene escape from the bustling city. With its central location, guests can explore the charming streets of the French Concession and indulge in the hotel's upscale amenities, including a rooftop pool and sophisticated dining options.

Location: 366 Shi Men Yi Road, Jing'an District, Shanghai, 200041, China
P**hone Number:** +86 21 3216 8199

Capella Shanghai, Jian Ye Li:

Nestled in the historic Xuhui District, Capella Shanghai, Jian Ye Li, offers a unique boutique experience within a restored shikumen (stone-gate) neighborhood. The hotel comprises luxurious villas with a fusion of classic Shanghainese and French design. Each villa is a private retreat, complete with a courtyard and personalized service. The location allows guests to immerse themselves in the charming ambiance of the French Concession while enjoying the exclusivity of Capella Shanghai.

Location: 480 West Jianguo Road, Xuhui **District, Shanghai,** 200031, China
Phone Number: +86 21 5466 9928

Urbn Hotel Shanghai:

Urbn Hotel Shanghai is an eco-friendly boutique stay located in the Jing'an District, bordering the French Concession. The hotel's industrial-chic design incorporates sustainable materials, creating a unique and environmentally conscious atmosphere. Urbn Hotel offers guests a serene escape with its cozy rooms, a rooftop terrace, and a commitment to eco-friendly practices. Its central location provides easy access to the trendy streets of the French Concession.

Location: 183 Jiaozhou Road, Jing'an District, Shanghai, 200040, China
Phone Number: +86 21 5153 4600

The Middle House offers chic and comfortable stays with contemporary design and excellent dining options in Shanghai's bustling Jing'an district. However, it may be expensive for budget travelers, some rooms may have limited views, and occasional noise disturbances could affect the overall guest experience.

Capella Shanghai in Jian Ye Li offers a unique stay in restored shikumen houses with personalized service and a tranquil ambiance. However, limited amenities, a remote location from central attractions, and pricey dining options may not suit guests seeking extensive facilities and budget-friendly dining.

URBN Hotel Shanghai offers eco-friendly accommodations with stylish and affordable rooms, prioritizing sustainability and comfort. However, its boutique size means limited amenities and potential noise disturbances from nearby urban activity, while basic services may not meet the expectations of guests accustomed to larger luxury hotels.

Budget-Friendly Hostels

Mingtown Etour Youth Hostel:

Nestled in the heart of the Huangpu District, Mingtown Etour Youth Hostel is a budget-friendly option for travelers seeking proximity to Shanghai's main attractions. With dormitory-style and private rooms, the hostel provides a comfortable and social environment. The location allows easy access to popular destinations like The Bund and People's Square. Mingtown Etour offers a range of budget options to suit different preferences.

Location: No.55 Jiangyin Road, Huangpu District, Shanghai, 200002, China
Phone Number: +86 21 6377 1123

Blue Mountain Bund Youth Hostel:

Situated near the iconic Bund, Blue Mountain Bund Youth Hostel combines affordability with a prime location. The hostel features cozy dormitories and private rooms with modern amenities. Guests can enjoy the vibrant atmosphere of the Huangpu District and easily explore nearby attractions. Blue Mountain Bund Youth Hostel provides a budget-friendly accommodation option with a social and laid-back ambiance.

Location: No. 30, Lane 130, East Beijing Road, Huangpu District, Shanghai, 200001, China
Phone Number: +86 21 6323 2598

Captain Hostel

Captain Hostel, centrally located in the Huangpu District, offers a budget-friendly stay with a nautical theme. The hostel provides dormitory-style rooms and private cabins, creating a unique and maritime-inspired atmosphere. With its proximity to The Bund and Nanjing Road, Captain Hostel is an ideal choice for budget-conscious travelers looking to explore Shanghai's main attractions.

Location: 37 Fuzhou Road, Huangpu District, Shanghai, 200002, China
Phone Number: +86 21 6333 4771

WHEN TO VISIT AND WEATHER

Shanghai's Climate

Spring (March to May): Spring in Shanghai is characterized by mild temperatures, with blossoming flowers and trees bringing color to the city. Temperatures typically range from 10°C to 20°C (50°F to 68°F). Spring is considered one of the best times to visit, as the weather is pleasant, and outdoor activities can be enjoyed.

Summer (June to August): Shanghai's summers are hot and humid, with temperatures ranging from 25°C to 35°C (77°F to 95°F). The city experiences occasional rain and high humidity levels. Summer is the peak tourist season, but visitors should be prepared for warm and muggy weather.

Autumn (September to November): Autumn brings cooler and more comfortable temperatures, ranging from 15°C to 25°C (59°F to 77°F). The season is marked by clear skies and a gradual decline in humidity. It's another favorable time for tourists to explore the city.

Winter (December to February): Winters in Shanghai are cool and damp, with temperatures ranging from 0°C to 10°C (32°F to 50°F). While snow is rare, occasional cold spells can occur. Winter is considered the off-peak season for tourism.

Rainfall: The city experiences a noticeable wet season during the summer months, with increased rainfall from June to August. Typhoons can also affect Shanghai during this period, leading to heavy rainfall and occasional storms.

Festival Calendar

Chinese New Year (Spring Festival):

Timing: Late January to early February (dates vary based on the lunar calendar)
The Chinese New Year marks the beginning of the lunar new year, and celebrations in Shanghai are a spectacle of vibrant parades, dragon dances, and elaborate fireworks. Traditional rituals, family gatherings, and the iconic lantern festival contribute to the festive atmosphere.

Lantern Festival:

Timing: 15th day of the first lunar month (usually in February)

Following Chinese New Year, the Lantern Festival illuminates Shanghai with an array of colorful lantern displays. People gather to appreciate the artistic lanterns, solve riddles attached to them, and enjoy performances and traditional snacks.

Shanghai International Film Festival:

Timing: June

A significant event in the global film industry, the Shanghai International Film Festival showcases a diverse selection of films from around the world. Film enthusiasts and industry professionals gather to participate in screenings, forums, and cultural exchanges.

Dragon Boat Festival:

Timing: 5th day of the 5th lunar month (usually in June)

The Dragon Boat Festival commemorates the ancient poet Qu Yuan. Dragon boat races, traditional zongzi (sticky rice dumplings) offerings, and colorful silk threads are common sights during this festival, adding cultural richness to Shanghai's summer.

Mid-Autumn Festival (Mooncake Festival):

Timing: 15th day of the 8th lunar month (usually in September)

The Mid-Autumn Festival is a time for family reunions and moon appreciation. Shanghai is adorned with lanterns, and families gather to share mooncakes, a symbolic treat. The cityscape is often aglow with colorful decorations.

Shanghai Tourism Festival:

Timing: September

Celebrating Shanghai as a global tourism destination, the Shanghai Tourism Festival features parades, cultural performances, and showcases the city's hospitality. Visitors can experience the diverse cultural heritage and attractions that make Shanghai a cosmopolitan metropolis.

Christmas and New Year's Eve:

Timing: December

While Christmas and New Year's Eve are not traditional Chinese festivals, Shanghai transforms into a winter wonderland during this time. The city is adorned with festive lights, and various events and celebrations take place in shopping districts, hotels, and entertainment venues.

Weather Tips for Different Times

Spring (March to May):
Tips: Pack layers, including a light jacket or sweater. Spring is one of the best times to visit Shanghai due to pleasant weather and blooming flowers.

Summer (June to August):
Tips: Wear lightweight and breathable clothing. Stay hydrated and be prepared for occasional rain. Consider carrying an umbrella and sunscreen.

Autumn (September to November):
Tips: Bring a mix of clothing for varying temperatures. Enjoy clear skies and comfortable weather for outdoor activities.

lWinter (December to February):
Tips: Pack warm layers, including a coat, hat, and gloves. While snow is rare, be prepared for occasional cold spells.

Rainy Season (June to August):
Tips: Carry an umbrella or raincoat. Check weather forecasts for potential typhoon alerts. Indoor activities and shopping districts are good options on rainy days.

GETTING AROUND SHANGHAI

Transportation Options

Metro: Shanghai's metro system is extensive, covering the city and its suburbs. It's a fast and economical way to travel, especially during rush hours when traffic congestion is common.
 Expenses: Metro tickets start at 3 RMB for short trips and vary based on distance. Consider purchasing a rechargeable transportation card for convenience and savings.
 Booking: Tickets can be purchased at metro stations, and transportation cards can be obtained and recharged at stations or convenience stores.

Buses: Shanghai's bus network is vast and reaches areas not covered by the metro. It's an economical option for exploring different neighborhoods.
 Expenses: Bus fares start at 2 RMB, and exact change is required. Transportation cards can also be used on buses for seamless travel.

Taxis: Taxis are readily available in Shanghai and are a convenient option, especially for those traveling with luggage or in a group.
 Expenses: Taxi fares start at 14 RMB, with additional charges based on distance. Prices may vary based on factors such as traffic and time of day.

DiDi (Ride-Sharing): DiDi is a popular ride-sharing app in Shanghai, providing a convenient and cost-effective alternative to traditional taxis.
 Expenses: DiDi fares are competitive, often similar to or slightly cheaper than taxis. Payment is made through the app.

Maglev Train: The Maglev Train connects Pudong International Airport to Longyang Road Metro Station, offering a high-speed transit option.
 Expenses: A one-way ticket costs 50 RMB, and round-trip tickets are available at a discount. The journey takes approximately 7 minutes.

Public Bicycles: Shanghai has a public bicycle system with bike stations throughout the city. It's an eco-friendly option for short-distance travel.
 Expenses: The first hour is typically free, and subsequent usage incurs a small fee. Registering through the bike-sharing app is required.

High-Speed Trains: For longer-distance travel, high-speed trains connect Shanghai with other major cities in China.
 Expenses: Ticket prices vary based on the destination and class of service. Booking in advance, especially during peak travel times, is advisable.

Ferries: Ferries operate across the Huangpu River, providing scenic views of the city's skyline.
 Expenses: Ferry fares are affordable, typically ranging from 2 to 12 RMB depending on the route.

Booking Tips:
 For metro, buses, and taxis, payment is usually made in cash. DiDi and some transportation cards allow for cashless transactions.
 High-speed train tickets can be booked online through official websites or mobile apps.

Renting Bicycles and Electric Scooters

Bicycles:

Choose a Service:
Shanghai offers several bike-sharing services, including Mobike, Ofo, and Hello Bike. Download the respective app for the service you choose.

Registration:
Register on the app by providing necessary details and linking a payment method. Some services may require a small deposit, which can be refunded upon account closure.

Locate Bikes:
Use the app to locate nearby available bicycles. Bikes are often scattered throughout the city and can be found near metro stations, bus stops, or popular landmarks.

Unlock and Ride:
Scan the QR code on the bike using the app to unlock it. Once unlocked, you are free to ride. Most services charge a per-minute rate, and payment is deducted from your account.

End the Ride:
Park the bike in designated areas, typically near sidewalks or bike racks. Lock the bike using the app to end the ride, and the fare is automatically calculated and deducted.

Electric Scooters:

Select an E-Scooter Service:
E-scooter services like Lime, Dott, and Hellobike offer electric scooters for rent. Download the app for the selected service.

Register and Verify:
Register on the app, provide necessary details, and verify your identity. Link a payment method to cover the cost of rides.

Locate E-Scooters:
Use the app to find nearby electric scooters. They are often parked at convenient locations, and their locations can be tracked in real-time.

Unlock and Ride:
Scan the QR code on the e-scooter using the app to unlock it. Electric scooters are typically charged per minute of usage, and the fare is calculated automatically.

End the Ride:
Park the e-scooter in designated areas, ensuring it doesn't obstruct pedestrian paths. Use the app to lock the scooter and end the ride, with the fare deducted from your account.

Essential Phrases for Communication

Greetings:
Hello: 你好 (Nǐ hǎo)
Goodbye: 再见 (Zàijiàn)
Common Courtesies:
Thank you: 谢谢 (Xièxiè)
Please: 请 (Qǐng)
Excuse me: 不好意思 (Bù hǎoyìsi)

Getting Around:
Where is...? : ...在哪里？ (... zài nǎlǐ?)
How much is this?: 这个多少钱？ (Zhège duōshǎo qián?)
I want to go to...: 我要去... (Wǒ yào qù...)

Dining:
Menu: 菜单 (Càidān)
I don't eat [ingredient]: 我不吃... (Wǒ bù chī...)
Delicious: 好吃 (Hǎo chī)

Shopping:
How much does this cost?: 这个多少钱？ (Zhège duōshǎo qián?)
Can you give me a discount?: 可以打折吗？ (Kěyǐ dǎzhé ma?)

Emergencies:
Help!: 救命！ (Jiùmìng!)
I need a doctor: 我需要看医生 (Wǒ xūyào kàn yīshēng)

Numbers:
1: 一 (Yī)
2: 二 (Èr)
3: 三 (Sān)
4: 四 (Sì)
5: 五 (Wǔ)
10: 十 (Shí)
100: 一百 (Yībǎi)
1000: 一千 (Yīqiān)

Time:
What time is it?: 现在几点？ (Xiànzài jǐ diǎn?)
Today: 今天 (Jīntiān)
Tomorrow: 明天 (Míngtiān)
Yesterday: 昨天 (Zuótiān)

Direction:
Where is the bathroom?: 厕所在哪里？ (Cèsuǒ zài nǎlǐ?)
Left: 左边 (Zuǒbiān)
Right: 右边 (Yòubiān)
Straight ahead: 往前走 (Wǎng qián zǒu)

Courtesy Expressions:
It's okay: 没关系 (Méi guānxi)
I'm sorry: 对不起 (Duìbuqǐ)
No problem: 没问题 (Méi wèntí)

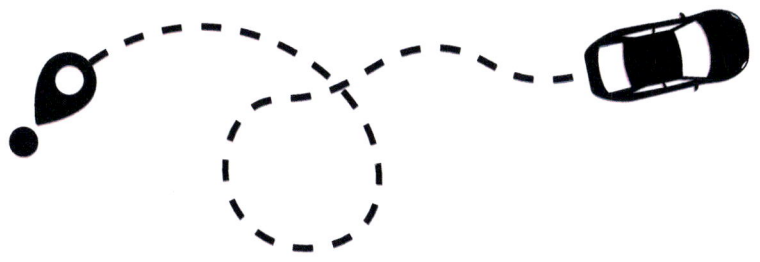

BEATING THE CROWDS

Best Times to Visit Popular Sites

The Bund and Pudong Skyline:
Best Time: Evening and Night
The mesmerizing city lights illuminate both sides of the Huangpu River, creating a stunning panorama. The dazzling skyline of Pudong, coupled with the historic architecture along The Bund, comes to life as darkness falls..

Shanghai Disney Resort:
Best Time: Weekdays, Off-Peak Seasons
To avoid large crowds and long queues, visit on weekdays and during off-peak seasons. This ensures a more enjoyable experience, shorter waiting times for rides, and easier navigation through the park.

Yuyuan Garden and Old Town:
Best Time: Early Morning
The serene atmosphere in the morning allows you to appreciate the classical beauty of Yuyuan Garden without the bustling crowds. Explore the charming Old Town streets as shops open, offering a peaceful start to your day.

The Former French Concession:
Best Time: Late Afternoon to Evening
Experience the laid-back charm of the Former French Concession during late afternoon and evening. Explore tree-lined avenues, trendy boutiques, and enjoy al fresco dining in this fashionable district.

Shanghai Tower and Jin Mao Tower:
Best Time: Clear Days with Good Visibility
For the most breathtaking views of Shanghai, visit the observation decks of Shanghai Tower and Jin Mao Tower on clear days. The cityscape and skyline are particularly spectacular during sunset and into the early evening.

Oriental Pearl Tower:
Best Time: Evening
The Oriental Pearl Tower dazzles at night with its colorful illumination. Enjoy the city lights and, if possible, catch the tower's light show, adding a magical touch to your evening.

Zhongshan Park:
Best Time: Spring and Autumn
The pleasant weather in spring and autumn makes these seasons ideal for a visit to Zhongshan Park. Enjoy blooming flowers in spring or colorful foliage in autumn as you stroll through this urban oasis.

Shanghai Museum:
Best Time: Weekdays, Morning
To avoid crowds and have a more leisurely exploration, visit the Shanghai Museum on weekdays, preferably in the morning. This allows you to appreciate the extensive collection of Chinese art and artifacts without the rush.

Insider Tips for Timing

Avoid Peak Tourist Seasons: Plan your visit during the shoulder seasons of spring (March to May) and autumn (September to November). These periods offer pleasant weather, fewer crowds, and a more relaxed atmosphere.

Early Mornings for Popular Attractions: Beat the crowds by visiting popular attractions early in the morning. Places like Yuyuan Garden and The Bund are more serene, allowing you to enjoy the beauty without jostling through crowds.

Weekdays Over Weekends: Opt for visiting attractions on weekdays, especially if you plan to explore museums, parks, or popular districts. This strategy helps avoid the weekend rush and provides a more peaceful experience.

Evenings for Skyline Views: Schedule visits to places like the Oriental Pearl Tower, Shanghai Tower, and Jin Mao Tower in the evening. The city lights and skyline become enchanting after sunset, creating a picturesque backdrop.

Lunchtime in Local Eateries: Experience authentic local cuisine by having lunch in popular local eateries. Locals typically dine around noon, so aim for lunchtime to savor delicious and freshly prepared dishes.

Night Markets and Street Food: Dive into the local culture by exploring night markets and trying street food. Late evenings are the best time to witness the vibrant street food scene, with stalls offering a variety of delectable treats.

Utilize Public Transportation Off-Peak: If using public transportation, plan your journeys during off-peak hours to avoid crowded metro cars and buses. This ensures a more comfortable and efficient commute.

Check Local Events Calendar: Before planning your trip, check the local events calendar for festivals, exhibitions, or cultural events. Participating in or witnessing local events can add a unique and memorable dimension to your visit.

Book Tickets in Advance: For popular attractions like Shanghai Disney Resort, consider booking tickets in advance to skip long queues and save time. This is particularly crucial during peak seasons.

Weather-Adapted Exploration: Shanghai experiences diverse weather conditions. Plan your daily activities based on the weather forecast. For instance, explore indoor attractions on rainy days and save outdoor adventures for clear skies

Reservation Strategies

Book Accommodations in Advance: Secure your accommodations well in advance, especially during peak seasons or major events. This ensures a wider range of options and potentially more favorable rates. Consider staying in centrally located areas for easy access to attractions.

Reserve Popular Attractions and Tours Online: Many popular attractions, museums, and tours in Shanghai offer online reservations. Booking in advance not only guarantees your entry but also often allows you to skip long queues, saving valuable time.

Plan Dining Reservations: For renowned or high-demand restaurants, particularly those in popular districts like the French Concession, consider making dining reservations. This is especially important for Michelin-starred establishments and popular local eateries. Apps or websites like Dianping or OpenTable can be handy for this.

Purchase Tickets for Entertainment in Advance: If you plan to attend shows, performances, or entertainment venues, purchase tickets in advance. This applies to places like acrobatic theaters, musical performances, and even some rooftop bars with panoramic views.

Secure Transportation Services Early: If you require transportation services such as airport transfers or private tours, consider booking them in advance. This ensures a hassle-free arrival and departure experience, especially if you have specific preferences or time constraints.

Utilize Mobile Apps for Transportation: Embrace mobile apps like Didi (China's version of Uber) for convenient and efficient transportation around the city. Booking rides in advance or at the moment of need becomes seamless, reducing wait times.

Check for Discounts and Packages: Before making reservations, explore available discounts or bundled packages. Many attractions, hotels, and services offer promotional rates or combo deals that can lead to cost savings.

Consider Guided Tours: For a more curated experience, consider joining guided tours. Many companies offer themed tours, walking tours, or even private guides who can provide insider insights. Booking such tours in advance ensures availability.

Flexible Reservation Policies: When making reservations for accommodations, tours, or other services, be aware of cancellation policies. Opt for options with flexible policies in case of unexpected changes to your travel plans.

Stay Informed About Local Events: Check local event calendars for festivals, exhibitions, or major events happening during your visit. Some events may require reservations, and being aware of them allows you to plan accordingly.

CULTURAL INSIGHTS AND ETIQUETTE

Understanding Local Customs

Greetings: In Shanghai, a friendly greeting is often accompanied by a nod or a slight bow. Handshakes are common in more formal settings, and many locals appreciate a simple "Nǐ hǎo" (你好), meaning "hello."

Respect for Elders: Confucian values emphasizing respect for elders are deeply ingrained in Chinese culture. When interacting with older individuals, a polite nod or a slight bow is a gesture of courtesy.

Gift Giving: Presenting a gift is a cherished custom, especially during festivals or social visits. When offering a gift, use both hands, and it's common for the recipient to politely refuse initially before accepting.

Tea Culture: Tea holds a special place in Chinese culture, and the act of pouring tea for others is a symbol of hospitality. When someone pours tea for you, tapping your fingers on the table is a way of expressing gratitude.

Dining Etiquette: Shanghai's culinary scene is a delight, and understanding dining etiquette is crucial. Wait for the host to start the meal, and it's customary to offer the best dishes to elders or guests first. Refusing food initially before accepting is considered polite.

Public Behavior: Maintaining a calm and composed demeanor in public is highly valued. Loud or disruptive behavior is generally frowned upon. Queueing in an orderly manner, especially in crowded places, is a sign of respect for others.

Shoes Indoors: It's customary to remove shoes when entering someone's home. Many traditional teahouses and restaurants may also require patrons to remove their shoes before entering certain areas.

Red Packets (Hóngbāo): During festive occasions, especially Chinese New Year, the custom of giving and receiving red packets filled with money is widespread. This symbolizes good luck and blessings for the recipient.

Paying the Bill: When dining out, the person who extends the invitation typically pays the bill. It's considered polite to offer to pay, but it's customary for the host to cover the expenses.

Dress Code and Behavior

Smart Casual Attire: Shanghai is a city where smart casual attire is generally well-received. Whether exploring the vibrant streets, dining in local eateries, or attending cultural events, wearing neat and presentable clothing is appropriate.

Formal Attire for Business: In business settings, a more formal dress code is expected. Business suits or professional attire are common, and attention to grooming and appearance is valued in corporate environments.

Conservative Dress in Traditional Settings: When visiting temples, traditional tea houses, or more conservative neighborhoods, it's advisable to dress modestly. Avoid overly revealing clothing to show respect for local customs.

Comfortable Footwear: Shanghai is a city made for walking, so comfortable footwear is essential. Whether exploring the bustling markets or strolling along the historic Bund, opt for shoes suitable for urban exploration.

Respect for Local Customs: Modesty and cultural sensitivity should guide your behavior. It's advisable to cover shoulders and knees when visiting religious sites or more traditional establishments, and remove your shoes when entering someone's home.

Umbrellas and Sun Protection: Shanghai's weather can be unpredictable, and it's common to see locals carrying umbrellas for sun protection. Carrying a light jacket or shawl is also practical, especially during cooler evenings.

Public Behavior: Maintaining a calm and collected demeanor in public is appreciated. Avoid loud conversations, especially in quiet places, and refrain from public displays of affection, as these may be considered inappropriate.

Queueing Etiquette: Queues are a part of daily life in Shanghai, especially in public transportation and popular attractions. Maintain order and respect personal space while waiting in lines.

Adapting to Local Styles: Shanghai is known for its fashion-forward locals. While dressing in a contemporary and stylish manner is generally accepted, it's also an opportunity to explore and incorporate some of the latest trends.

Interacting with Locals

Learn Basic Mandarin Phrases: While many locals in Shanghai may speak English, making an effort to learn basic Mandarin phrases demonstrates respect for the local culture. Simple greetings like "nǐ hǎo" (你好 - hello) and "xièxiè" (谢谢 - thank you) can go a long way.

Smile and Maintain Politeness: A warm smile is universally understood, and Shanghai locals appreciate politeness. Addressing people with "nǐ" (you) and using courteous language fosters a friendly atmosphere.

Participate in Local Customs: Embracing local customs and traditions helps you connect with locals on a deeper level. Participate in festivals, visit traditional teahouses, or explore local markets to experience daily life.

Respect Personal Space: While Shanghai is a bustling metropolis, respecting personal space is essential. Maintain a comfortable distance when conversing, especially with strangers, to avoid making anyone uncomfortable.

Be Open to Cultural Exchange: Locals in Shanghai often appreciate cultural exchange. Engage in conversations about your own culture and show genuine interest in learning about theirs. This openness fosters mutual understanding.

Use Social Media and Translation Apps: Platforms like WeChat are widely used in China. Having a WeChat account can facilitate communication and connections. Additionally, translation apps can assist in bridging language barriers.

Join Local Events and Meetups: Attend local events, meetups, or language exchange sessions. This provides an opportunity to meet both expats and locals who share common interests, fostering connections in a relaxed setting.

Explore Local Hangouts: Venture beyond tourist hotspots and explore local hangouts. Whether it's a traditional tea house, a community park, or a neighborhood eatery, these places offer a more authentic glimpse into daily life.

Be Mindful of Cultural Sensitivities: Awareness of cultural sensitivities is crucial. Topics like politics and personal finances may be sensitive, so it's advisable to steer clear of potentially contentious subjects.

SHANGHAI'S HISTORICAL BACKGROUND

Early Settlements and Trade

Early Settlements:

The earliest evidence of human settlement in the Shanghai area dates back to the Neolithic period, around 6,000 years ago. Archaeological findings suggest that the region was inhabited by fishing communities and agricultural societies. As time progressed, Shanghai became a center for the cultivation of rice and other crops, establishing the foundations for a settled community.

During the Ming Dynasty (1368-1644), Shanghai began to take on a more urbanized character. The construction of city walls and the establishment of local government structures marked a transition from a primarily agricultural region to a more organized settlement. However, it was during the Qing Dynasty (1644-1912) that Shanghai truly began to flourish as a commercial and trading hub.

Trade History:

The strategic location of Shanghai at the confluence of the Yangtze River and the East China Sea made it a natural gateway for trade. During the Ming and Qing Dynasties, Shanghai became an essential market for agricultural products, silk, and handicrafts from the surrounding regions. The city's proximity to the Grand Canal, which connected northern and southern China, further enhanced its role in trade.

The Opium Wars in the mid-19th century marked a turning point for Shanghai's trade history. After the signing of the Treaty of Nanking in 1842, Shanghai was designated as one of the treaty ports, opening it up to foreign trade. The city quickly transformed into an international settlement, attracting traders, merchants, and entrepreneurs from various Western countries.

The establishment of the Shanghai International Settlement and the French Concession in the late 19th and early 20th centuries further fueled the city's economic growth. Foreign powers set up their own districts within Shanghai, creating a cosmopolitan and diverse urban environment.

The Bund, a waterfront area along the Huangpu River, became the financial and commercial heart of the city, lined with iconic European-style buildings.

In the early 20th century, Shanghai emerged as a global financial and trading center. The city played a crucial role in facilitating trade between China and the rest of the world. However, political instability and the Japanese occupation during World War II interrupted this growth.

After the establishment of the People's Republic of China in 1949, Shanghai experienced a period of economic decline. However, with the initiation of economic reforms in the late 20th century, the city once again became a powerhouse for trade and commerce. Today, Shanghai stands as one of the world's major financial centers and continues to play a pivotal role in global trade and economic development.

The earliest evidence of human settlement in the Shanghai area dates back to the Neolithic period, around 6,000 years ago. Archaeological findings suggest that the region was inhabited by fishing communities and agricultural societies.

As time progressed, Shanghai became a center for the cultivation of rice and other crops, establishing the foundations for a settled community.

During the Ming Dynasty (1368-1644), Shanghai began to take on a more urbanized character. The construction of city walls and the establishment of local government structures marked a transition from a primarily agricultural region to a more organized settlement. However, it was during the Qing Dynasty (1644-1912) that Shanghai truly began to flourish as a commercial and trading hub.

Colonial Influences

Treaty of Nanking and Foreign Concessions (1842): The Treaty of Nanking, signed in 1842 after the First Opium War, opened up several Chinese ports to foreign trade. Shanghai became one of the primary treaty ports, allowing foreign powers to establish settlements and concessions. The British, Americans, French, and other European nations gained extraterritorial rights in designated areas of the city.

International Settlement: The Shanghai International Settlement, established in 1863, was a joint administrative region governed by representatives from Britain, the United States, and other Western nations. This area, located in the northern part of the city, became a cosmopolitan enclave with its own legal and economic systems. The International Settlement played a crucial role in shaping Shanghai's modernization and economic development.

French Concession: In addition to the International Settlement, the French Concession was established in 1849 and expanded in 1862. The French influence brought a distinct European flavor to Shanghai, with tree-lined boulevards, colonial-style architecture, and a vibrant cultural scene. The French Concession operated under French law, and its unique character still influences the cityscape today.

British Influence: The British played a significant role in Shanghai's colonial history, particularly in the establishment of the International Settlement. The Bund, a waterfront area along the Huangpu River, became a symbol of British and international financial power. Many iconic buildings along the Bund, such as the Peace Hotel, showcase British colonial architectural influences.

Cultural Exchange: The foreign concessions in Shanghai became melting pots of cultural exchange. Western businesses, schools, and social institutions coexisted with Chinese counterparts, fostering a unique blend of Eastern and Western cultures. This cultural fusion is still evident in Shanghai's diverse culinary scene, architecture, and lifestyle.

Economic Development: The colonial period significantly contributed to Shanghai's economic development. The city became a major financial and trading hub, connecting China with the global economy. Foreign businesses and banks set up operations in the concessions, turning Shanghai into a center for finance, commerce, and industry.

World War II and Post-Colonial Period: During World War II, Shanghai experienced Japanese occupation, leading to the decline of foreign influence. After the war, the Chinese government gradually regained control over the concessions, culminating in their complete dissolution in 1949 with the establishment of the People's Republic of China.

Revolutionary Period

May Fourth Movement (1919): The seeds of political change were sown during the May Fourth Movement, which originated in response to the Treaty of Versailles and the perceived betrayal of Chinese interests. In Shanghai, intellectuals, students, and workers joined protests, demanding political reform, cultural renewal, and an end to foreign concessions. This movement laid the groundwork for future revolutionary activities.

Nationalist Movement and Republic of China (1911-1949): The overthrow of the Qing Dynasty in 1911 marked the establishment of the Republic of China. Shanghai played a crucial role during this period as a major center for political, economic, and cultural activities. The city became a focal point for both Nationalist (Kuomintang, or KMT) and Communist activities, with various factions vying for control.

Shanghai Massacre (1927): The alliance between the Nationalists and Communists, forged during the Northern Expedition against warlords, collapsed in 1927. In Shanghai, the KMT-led government conducted a brutal purge known as the Shanghai Massacre, targeting Communists and left-wing activists. This event led to a significant loss for the Communist movement in the city.

Shanghai as a Revolutionary Base (1927-1937): Despite the setbacks, Shanghai remained a center for revolutionary activities. The CCP, led by figures like Zhou Enlai, operated clandestinely in the city, organizing labor movements and anti-imperialist protests. The Red Trade Union, an underground organization, played a crucial role in mobilizing workers and peasants.

Japanese Occupation (1937-1945): The outbreak of the Second Sino-Japanese War in 1937 saw the Japanese occupation of Shanghai. The city suffered greatly during this period, with widespread atrocities and the establishment of a puppet government. The Communist and Nationalist forces suspended their internal conflict to focus on resisting the Japanese invaders, setting the stage for future cooperation during the later stages of World War II.

Liberation of Shanghai (1949): As World War II came to an end, the Nationalists and Communists resumed their struggle for control.

The Communist forces, led by the People's Liberation Army (PLA), launched a successful offensive to liberate Shanghai from Nationalist rule in 1949. On May 27, 1949, the city officially fell to the Communists, marking a crucial victory in the establishment of the People's Republic of China.

Modern Economic Development

Economic Reforms (Late 20th Century): China, under the leadership of Deng Xiaoping, embarked on a series of economic reforms in the late 1970s, transitioning from a centrally planned economy to a more market-oriented system. Shanghai, with its historical legacy as a trading hub, was identified as a key player in this economic revitalization.

Pudong Development: One of the most significant initiatives was the development of Pudong, the area east of the Huangpu River. In 1990, the Chinese government declared Pudong a Special Economic Zone (SEZ) and designated it as a focus for financial and economic development. This decision led to a dramatic transformation of the Pudong skyline, with the construction of iconic skyscrapers, such as the Oriental Pearl Tower and the Shanghai World Financial Center.

Financial Center and Trade Hub: Shanghai's strategic location as a major port and its historical role in trade made it a natural choice for the development of a global financial center. The Lujiazui Financial District in Pudong became the heart of Shanghai's financial activities, housing the Shanghai Stock Exchange and numerous multinational corporations. The city's role as a trade hub was further strengthened by the development of the Yangshan Deep-Water Port, one of the world's largest container ports.

Free-Trade Zone (FTZ): In 2013, the Shanghai FTZ was established, covering a significant area including parts of Pudong. The FTZ aimed to promote economic liberalization, allowing for greater foreign investment and trade facilitation. It served as an experimental ground for testing financial and trade reforms, attracting multinational companies looking to establish a presence in China.

Innovation and Technology Hub: Shanghai has increasingly focused on becoming a hub for innovation and technology. The Zhangjiang Hi-Tech Park in Pudong has attracted numerous research institutions, tech companies, and startups. The city's commitment to fostering innovation is reflected in initiatives such as the "Made in Shanghai" plan, emphasizing advanced manufacturing and technological development.

Cultural and Entertainment Industry: Beyond finance and technology, Shanghai has invested in developing its cultural and entertainment industries. The city hosts international events, such as the Shanghai International Film Festival, and has become a prominent destination for tourism and cultural exchange. Areas like Xintiandi and the Former French Concession showcase a blend of historical charm and modern lifestyle.

Global City Status: Shanghai's economic development has propelled it to global city status, alongside international metropolises like New York, London, and Tokyo. The city's openness to foreign investment, its modern infrastructure, and its vibrant cultural scene contribute to its standing as a global economic and cultural hub.

ARCHITECTURAL DIVERSITY

Colonial-Era Buildings

European Styles:

Neo-Classical: Many buildings in the former International Settlement and French Concession exhibit Neo-Classical architecture. The Bund, in particular, features structures like the Customs House and the Shanghai Club, with columns, grand facades, and symmetrical designs reminiscent of classical European architecture.

Gothic Revival: Some colonial-era buildings in Shanghai showcase Gothic Revival elements, characterized by pointed arches, ribbed vaults, and flying buttresses. St. Ignatius Cathedral in Xujiahui is a notable example, combining Gothic and Romanesque styles.

Art Deco:

The Bund's Art Deco Buildings: As Shanghai entered the early 20th century, Art Deco gained popularity. Several buildings along the Bund, such as the Bank of China Building and the Peace Hotel, feature sleek lines, geometric patterns, and decorative motifs typical of the Art Deco style.

Tudor Revival:

Villas in the Former French Concession: In the former French Concession, you can find Tudor Revival-style villas with steeply pitched roofs, half-timbering, and decorative chimneys. These structures often blend European aesthetics with a touch of local influence, creating a distinctive architectural fusion.

Shikumen Architecture:

Traditional Chinese and Western Blend: Shikumen houses, prevalent in Shanghai's older neighborhoods, reflect a combination of Chinese and Western architectural elements. These narrow stone-gated lane houses often feature brick or stone facades with Western-style arched doorways.

Beaux-Arts:

Custom House and Shanghai Art Museum: Beaux-Arts architecture, characterized by grandiosity and classical symmetry, is evident in buildings like the Custom House on the Bund and the former Shanghai Art Museum (now the China Art Museum). The latter combines Beaux-Arts with Renaissance elements.

Spanish and Mediterranean Influences:
Garden Villas: Some villas in Shanghai, especially those in the Hongqiao area, exhibit Spanish or Mediterranean influences. These structures often boast terracotta roofs, arched windows, and decorative ironwork.

Modernist and International Style:
1950s and 1960s Buildings: Post-1949, Shanghai witnessed the construction of buildings influenced by Modernist and International styles. The Broadway Mansion is an example, featuring streamlined designs and functional aesthetics.

Art Deco and Modern Structures

Peace Hotel: The Peace Hotel, located on the Bund, is an iconic Art Deco building that stands as a testament to Shanghai's cosmopolitan past. Built in 1929, it features a distinctive green copper roof, symmetrical patterns, and intricate decorative elements.

Customs House: The Customs House on the Bund is another Art Deco gem, known for its impressive clock tower and geometric ornamentation. Completed in 1927, it exemplifies the elegance and modernity associated with Art Deco architecture.

Bank of China Building: Built in 1937, the Bank of China Building on the Bund is a striking example of Art Deco design.

Its stepped form, ornate detailing, and the use of decorative elements make it a prominent landmark along the waterfront.

Park Hotel: The Park Hotel, completed in 1934, is one of Shanghai's tallest Art Deco buildings. Its distinctive green pyramid roof and geometric patterns contribute to its unique architectural identity.

Metropole Hotel: The Metropole Hotel, now the Fairmont Peace Hotel, showcases Art Deco influences in its design. Opened in 1929, it boasts a distinctive facade, elegant interiors, and period-specific detailing.

Modern Structures:

Jin Mao Tower: A symbol of modern Shanghai, the Jin Mao Tower is a skyscraper in the Lujiazui area of Pudong. Completed in 1999, it combines modernist and traditional Chinese architectural elements, standing as one of the city's tallest structures.

Shanghai World Financial Center: Adjacent to the Jin Mao Tower, the Shanghai World Financial Center is an iconic modern skyscraper. Completed in 2008, its distinctive trapezoidal aperture at the top makes it a recognizable part of the city's skyline.

Shanghai Tower: The Shanghai Tower, completed in 2015, is the tallest of the trio in Lujiazui. Its spiral design and sustainable features contribute to its significance in contemporary architecture.

Shanghai Oriental Art Center: Opened in 2005, the Shanghai Oriental Art Center in Pudong is a modern cultural venue with a distinctive shell-like roof. The design combines innovative architecture with functional spaces for various performing arts.

Shanghai Natural History Museum: Designed by the renowned architect Ralph Appelbaum, the Shanghai Natural History Museum, opened in 2015, features a contemporary design that incorporates sustainable elements. The building's facade resembles a giant rock, harmonizing with its surroundings.

Arts and Culture Scene

Shanghai's International Confluence: Shanghai's historical role as an international port and a center for trade and cultural exchange has influenced its literary landscape. Writers from both China and abroad have been drawn to the city, seeking inspiration from its vibrant atmosphere, diverse population, and dynamic history.

The Golden Age of Shanghai Literature (1920s-1940s): The early to mid-20th century is often referred to as the "Golden Age" of Shanghai literature. During this period, the city witnessed a flourishing of literary movements, including the New Culture Movement and the creation of influential literary journals such as "Xinyue" (New Monthly) and "Shenbao" (The Shanghai Evening Post).

Prominent Literary Figures: Renowned Chinese writers, such as Lu Xun, Ba Jin, and Eileen Chang, have connections to Shanghai. Lu Xun, often considered the father of modern Chinese literature, spent significant time in the city and wrote some of his most influential works there.

The Shanghai Literary Scene Today: Contemporary Shanghai continues to be a vibrant hub for literature. The city hosts literary festivals, book fairs, and author events that attract both local and international writers. Literary organizations and writing groups contribute to the ongoing development of Shanghai's literary scene.

Old Shanghai Literary Cafes: Literary cafes have been integral to Shanghai's intellectual life for decades. Old literary cafes, such as the legendary Paramount, once frequented by writers and artists in the 1930s, have left an indelible mark on the city's cultural history.

Mao Dun Literary Bookstore: Named after the prominent Chinese writer Mao Dun, this literary bookstore and cafe has been a cultural institution since the 1930s. Located in the former French Concession, it provides a cozy space for book lovers and has hosted numerous literary events over the years.

Deli Lane: Deli Lane, situated in the Xintiandi district, is a popular literary cafe known for its relaxed ambiance and book-lined shelves. It attracts both locals and expatriates, offering a quiet retreat for reading and writing.

Sculpting in Time Bookstore Café: Located in the Jing'an District, this bookstore cafe draws inspiration from Andrei Tarkovsky's film "Sculpting in Time." It provides a serene environment for literary enthusiasts to enjoy books and engage in discussions.

Duoyun Books: Duoyun Books, nestled in the former French Concession, is a cultural space that combines a bookstore, cafe, and art gallery. It often hosts literary events, creating a dynamic platform for writers and readers to connect.

Co-working Spaces with Literary Themes: Some modern co-working spaces in Shanghai incorporate literary themes, providing a contemporary twist to the traditional literary cafe. These spaces offer a blend of creative work environments, coffee culture, and literary events.

RELIGIOUS AND SPIRITUAL HERITAGE

Temples and Shrines

Jade Buddha Temple:

Founded in 1882, the Jade Buddha Temple (Yufo Si) is one of Shanghai's most famous Buddhist temples. It houses two jade Buddha statues brought from Burma – the Sitting Buddha and the Recumbent Buddha. The temple is an oasis of tranquility amid the bustling city.

The architecture of the Jade Buddha Temple reflects the Song Dynasty style. Intricate carvings, traditional roofs with upturned eaves, and serene courtyards create a contemplative atmosphere. Visitors can explore various halls, pagodas, and beautiful gardens within the temple complex.

Longhua Temple:

Longhua Temple, with a history dating back over 1,700 years, is the oldest and largest Buddhist temple in Shanghai. Originally built in the Three Kingdoms period, it has been reconstructed multiple times. The temple complex includes a pagoda, bell tower, and several halls.

The architectural style of Longhua Temple represents classic Chinese design with pagodas, bridges, and courtyards. The grand Hall of Heavenly Kings, the Mahavira Hall, and the Jade Buddha Tower are among its prominent structures. The temple's serene garden, adorned with stone bridges and ponds, provides a peaceful retreat.

City God Temple (Chenghuang Miao):

The City God Temple, located in the heart of the Old City, is dedicated to the three city gods of Shanghai. It has been a spiritual and cultural hub for locals for centuries, serving as a place for worship, commerce, and community activities.

The temple complex includes various halls, altars, and pavilions. It hosts traditional ceremonies and festivals, including the Temple Fair during the Chinese New Year. The surrounding Yu Garden and bazaar contribute to the vibrant cultural atmosphere of the area.

Jing'an Temple:

Jing'an Temple, originally built in 247 AD, has undergone several reconstructions. The current structure, however, is a harmonious blend of traditional and modern elements. Its gold-plated Burmese jade statue of Buddha is a prominent attraction.

The temple grounds include halls, gardens, and the modern Jing'an Sculpture Park. It has become not only a spiritual center but also a cultural space hosting art exhibitions, performances, and cultural events.

Xiaotaoyuan Mosque:

Xiaotaoyuan Mosque, located in the Xiaotaoyuan area, is one of Shanghai's oldest and largest mosques. It serves as a religious center for the city's Muslim community and stands as a testament to Shanghai's religious diversity.

The mosque's architecture reflects a blend of traditional Chinese and Islamic styles. The prayer hall, minaret, and courtyard showcase intricate designs and patterns, creating a serene environment for worship.
Cultural and Spiritual Preservation:

Cultural Practices:

Temples and shrines in Shanghai are not merely historic relics but continue to be active centers of religious practices and cultural activities. Regular rituals, festivals, and ceremonies are conducted, allowing visitors to witness and participate in traditional customs.

The local government and religious communities work together to preserve and protect these cultural and spiritual heritage sites. Restoration projects, educational initiatives, and cultural events contribute to the ongoing vitality of these sacred places.

Printed in Great Britain
by Amazon